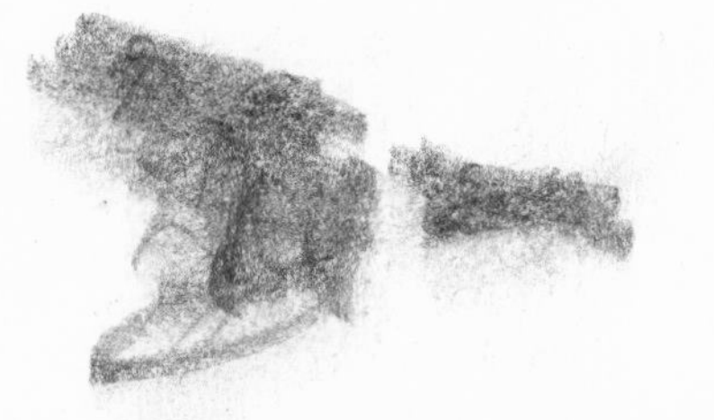

PRACTICAL FISHING KNOTS

Lefty Kreh
•
Mark Sosin

PRACTICAL FISHING KNOTS

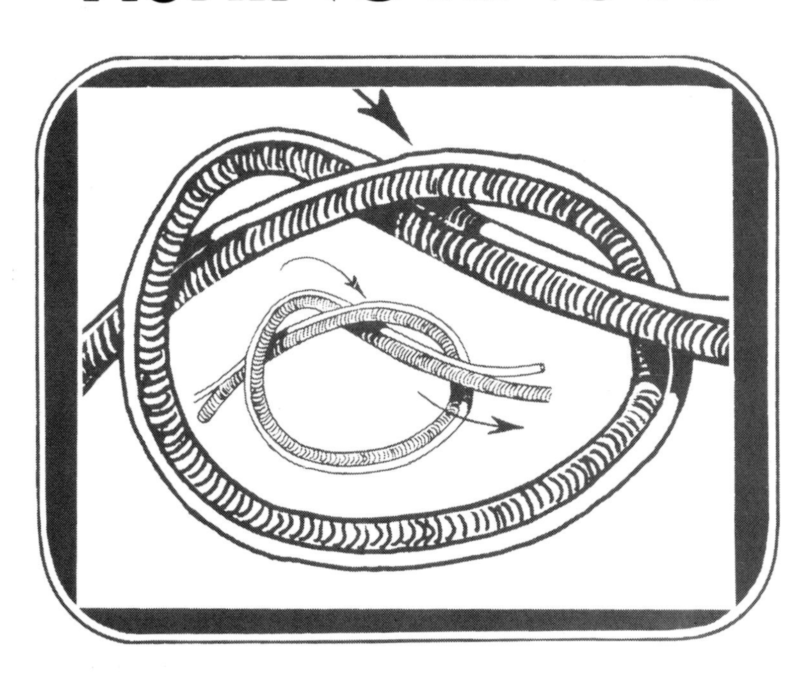

CROWN PUBLISHERS, INC., NEW YORK

ACKNOWLEDGMENTS

TO SINGLE out each individual who contributed to this book would be an impossible task, because the information presented spans over sixty years of combined fishing effort. During that period, we have fished many of the world's waters with many of the best anglers of our time. To each of them we owe a debt of gratitude for his capable assistance in helping us to learn more about knots and lines.

An extra measure of appreciation is extended to those fishermen (many of whom are close friends) who have been innovators of knots and were willing to help satiate our thirst for knowledge by sharing their discoveries with us.

We would be remiss if we did not acknowledge the valuable and vital technical assistance supplied by R. Howard Payne and the entire staff at the Filaments Division, E. I. du Pont de Nemours. They graciously opened the files to their many years of detailed research on knots and monofilament lines.

The line drawings were prepared by Neil Kenny and we extend our hand to him for his herculean efforts in the face of staggering deadlines.

Finally, a special measure of gratitude and heartfelt thanks goes to Nick Lyons, our talented editor, who helped us conceive this idea, encouraged us along the way, and worked diligently with us to bring this book to fruition.

Library of Congress Catalog Card Number: 72–84294
ISBN: 0–517–500418
Printed in the United States of America
Published simultaneously in Canada by General Publishing Company Limited

PREFACE

TWO THINGS have become overwhelmingly apparent to us after many years of teaching knot tying to individuals and groups of anglers across the United States and on the shores of foreign waters—most fishermen know very little about knots and even less about fishing lines, but most fishermen harbor an absorbing desire to master (or at least become proficient in) this vital subject. In the past, anglers faced the dilemma of where to find the needed information. Nothing in the archives of angling literature has treated knots and lines with any degree of completeness. Many anglers have clipped articles from magazines, hoarded pamphlets from line manufacturers, or dog-eared the pages in a book that demonstrated a knot or two. But the latest innovations were seldom published in any form and the illustrations used for the basic knots were frequently confusing, forcing the angler to struggle and often abandon the project.

There are thousands of knots in use by fishermen today. Yet, only a handful of these could pass the rigid scrutiny and demanding exactness of top-rated anglers. Most fishermen have heard of these knots by name, but have no way of learning to tie them.

We have called this book *Practical Fishing Knots* so that we could eliminate those ties that we consider nonessential and concentrate our efforts on detailing only the critical knots for the reader. We have chosen to demonstrate most of the knots with step-by-step photographs, just as if you were looking over the shoulder of the tyer. Artwork has been used only where the hand positions while tying would cover the knot. The instructions are comprehensive—maybe even too comprehensive—but we didn't want to overlook a single detail.

Once you learn to tie a representative sample of the knots we have presented, you'll be qualified to rig tackle for any fishing situation. But we owe you a word of warning. Your friends are going to come to you for help in tying knots, and before long you can also expect their friends to be knocking at your door.

A good craftsman not only knows the procedure for working with a chosen material, but he understands the properties of that material as well. It's no different with knots and lines. The two are so delicately intertwined that knowledge of one begs information about the other. To present the total picture, we have included a wealth of little-known data about fishing lines with particular emphasis on the popular, but ironically mysterious monofilament. We urge you to study and evaluate this section before you unspool a length of line and tie any of the knots. When you are finished, we sincerely hope that you will know a little more about the critical subject of fishing lines and knots than when you started.

LEFTY KREH
MARK SOSIN

CONTENTS

PRACTICAL FISHING KNOTS

1 THE IMPORTANCE OF KNOTS

Is it possible to be a really successful angler without becoming proficient in tying knots and understanding the properties of fishing lines? The top fishermen in the world don't think so. They are so adamant about good knots that they flatly refuse to let anyone else tie knots for them. Are they merely being arbitrary, or do they know something that most fishermen overlook? If you were to ask the men who consistently perform outstanding angling feats, they would tell you that being able to tie the right knots correctly is vital to hooking and landing fish successfully.

With a little practice, knot tying is easy. In fact, it is often easier to tie a good knot than a poor one. For one thing, you won't have to waste time trying to figure out how to join two pieces of line or how to put the right loop in the end; and, once you master the skills of knot tying, you will become a more competent fisherman. More fish are lost because of improperly tied knots or inattention to fishing lines than for all other reasons combined. There's little question that the trophy that got away either broke the line or a knot gave out.

A knot is nothing more than a connection. It can be a connection in the line itself, between two lines, between line and leader, or for attaching a lure, hook, swivel, or sinker; it is a link that can be used to join lines of similar or dissimilar diameters and materials or attach something to the end of the line. Every knot does not suit every purpose. The secret is in knowing what knot to use and when to use it.

Poor Knots

Poor knots have several common characteristics. They are generally too weak for the situation, drawn up incorrectly, and badly trimmed. A poor knot may be nothing more than the wrong knot for a particular application. Bulky knots that won't pass through the guides on the rod or offer a tempting target in the water for other fish to strike are poor. And, if you have to burn the end of monofilament to stop a knot from slipping, you can be sure it's not properly tied. Burning or the heat from a flame can easily damage both the knot and the line. You are also failing to construct knots properly if you have to tie an overhand knot in the end to prevent slippage.

Good Knots

In monofilament, a good knot is one that does not slip. All knots in monofilament start to slip just before they break. Generally speaking, however, a good knot is the proper knot for a particular situation—one with enough strength to meet the fishing conditions. It must be neat, correctly trimmed, and boast sufficient knot strength. Sometimes, a good knot may be the fastest one to tie under certain circumstances; if you have to re-rig while a school of fish is playing havoc with the surface of the water, you might not have time to tie the best knot, but you do want to be able to tie a good knot quickly.

To fight a fish effectively, you must apply the maximum pressure that the tackle can withstand. The amount of pressure is usually dictated by the breaking strength of the line. And the unknotted breaking strength of the line can be weakened by incorrect or poorly tied knots. That means that most fishermen have no idea how much pressure it takes to break a line that has been knotted. Without this vital information, there is no way in which they can fight a fish to the maximum. Chances are that a knot will break before the rated breaking strength of the line.

On the other hand, some knots are rated equal to the unknotted line strength and, by using these or by using combinations of knots, an angler can learn through experience just how much pressure he can put on a fish.

Equally important, good knots are easy to tie and can be fashioned quickly. The angler who casually selects a knot is stacking the deck against himself even before he hooks a fish. The angler, however, who appreciates the value of a good knot seldom has to tell the age-old story of the fish that got away.

Even veterans become careless at times and in the haste of the moment exhibit a tendency to cut corners. Something becomes "good enough" rather than the best for the circumstances. Invariably, taking a shortcut when it comes to knot tying proves to be a costly endeavor, and the price of the error is another lost fish (plus the terminal tackle). In selecting the proper knot for a given situation, the first step is to analyze what you are trying to achieve; then select the best knot for the job *that you can tie well.* If you can't tie a specific knot, it is no good for your purposes. Remember: there is no need to use elaborate knots just because you can tie them when simple knots will do the job.

Knot Materials

In order to satisfy the requirements as a fishing line, any material used must be capable of holding knots; the same applies to leader material. The most popular type of line in use today for fishing and for leaders is monofilament—a single strand of nylon available in a wide variety of breaking strengths. However, some fishing situations will dictate the use of braided nylon or Dacron line; others will require fly line, lead core, or even Monel wire. Leader material also runs through a wide range stretching from monofilament through coated and uncoated braided wire, solid wire, and even aircraft cable. It is important to remember that each type of material requires special knots and that not every knot will perform satisfactorily in each type of material.

Learning to Tie Knots

The only place to learn how to tie a specific knot correctly is in the relaxed atmosphere ashore. If you wait until you are on the water in a fishing situation, you're almost certain to succumb to the frustrations of the moment and the results will be less than satisfactory. And you will wrongly, but quickly, decide that the knot you are attempting is too complicated in the first place —or you'll convince yourself that you can "get by" with a less-than-adequate knot.

Ashore, at your leisure, you can take your time and master the quickest and easiest method for tying a knot. You will also have ample time to practice. Remember that by practicing a knot, you will gain speed in tying it and achieve a degree of uniformity that is of paramount importance. The goal in knot tying is consistency. If a knot is tied poorly or incorrectly, it should be retied immediately. In fact, experts who tie knots for laboratory testing often practice on a particular knot for a half hour or more before they submit samples for the actual testing.

Even when you have mastered a particular knot, it is always best to rig your tackle ashore and in advance of any fishing excursion. Experts will tell you that most big fish are caught *the night before.* They are referring specifically to tackle preparation and knot tying. If you have extra spools for your spinning reels, for example, leaders should be attached to each one before you go fishing. Then, when you change spools, all the knots are in place and you merely have to rig up a rod and tie a lure or hook on the end.

Finally, you can determine the breaking strength of a particular knot through a simple procedure. Secure the line with the knot to an empty bucket and attach the other end to something rigid so that the bucket hangs suspended an inch or two off the ground. Slowly fill the bucket with sand or water. When the knot breaks, weigh the bucket on an ordinary scale and you have the breaking strength of the knot. Try this test several times on the same type knot and you'll know if you are achieving consistency in your tying.

Recognize from the beginning that not everyone can tie *all* knots well. There are bound to be a few knots that will seem difficult at first, so bypass these until you master the others. The best procedure is to select one or two knots for the various fishing situations and concentrate on them. Then you can go back and learn the others. You only have to be able to tie a few knots to satisfy most fishing requirements. The key is how well you can tie these knots rather than how many different knots you can tie.

We cannot emphasize enough that the place to learn a new knot is at home and not on the water. Don't use a knot in a fishing situation until you can tie it comfortably and without struggling. It is far better to tie a poor knot well than a good knot poorly. And finally, like learning a foreign language, you cannot master knot tying unless you are willing to practice, practice, and practice some more.

2 MONOFILAMENT LINE

CONTRARY to the belief of some fishermen, nylon monofilament fishing line does not last forever. After a certain period of time, it begins to lose some of the properties that it had when it was new, resulting in a reduction of breaking strength. You might think you are using ten-pound test, but in actuality, you may have only eight-pound test on your spool because of deterioration.

All monofilament lines should be inspected frequently for signs of wear. If the line is frayed, that's your first clue that it should be changed. Frayed line is always much weaker than the original and it can result from grooved or chipped guides on the rod, a roller that fails to turn under pressure on a spinning reel, or by being rubbed across bottom obstructions such as rocks or coral while fighting a fish. If the frayed portion doesn't extend too far back in the line, you can simply cut it off and retie your terminal tackle. But if removal of the frayed portion considerably reduces the amount of line on the spool, invest in a new line.

Inspect your line for stiffness and brittleness. Line that has been on a reel too long loses certain additives in the nylon and it has an almost wiry feel to it. Compare it to new line of the same make and breaking strength if you have any doubts. If the line is much stiffer than the original, it should be replaced.

Usually, the end of the line receives the hardest use and is the first part to deteriorate. On relatively light lines (under twenty-pound test), try breaking the line in your hands by snapping your hands apart. Be careful to protect your hands from line cuts by wrapping them with a handkerchief or by wearing gloves. If the line breaks easily, keep stripping it off the reel and trying to break it until you find a stronger portion. The difference in the breaking strength should be totally obvious.

When you do find a stronger portion, tie an overhand knot in it and try breaking it. If the line still breaks easily, you should discard the line and replace it with new.

We mentioned earlier that you can use a bucket with sand or water to test the breaking strength of a knot; the same procedure can be used to determine the breaking strength of line. In fact, when you spool new line on a reel, it's a good practice to run these tests a few times and obtain an average breaking strength for the new line. This could be marked somewhere on the spool of the reel and later compared to subsequent tests when you are trying to find out if the line is still usable.

When to Change Line

Veteran fishermen change lines frequently and consider new monofilament to be the most effective and inexpensive insurance they can buy for landing fish consistently. Some will even change line after a single fish if the battle was a tough one and they are not sure the line hasn't been weakened through abrasion. Most fishermen, however, have an aversion to changing monofilament lines until someone comes along and convinces them that it has seriously deteriorated.

As a general rule, monofilament line should be changed at least twice as often as you currently believe it should be changed, and certainly at least once a year if you've done an average amount of fishing. If you've done some hard fishing—particularly in salt water—the line may have to be changed as often as every few days. This sounds hard to believe, but the serious fisherman is more concerned with his line and knots than most other aspects of tackle. If you're going to put your tackle to the test on a good fish, the line is critical. Compared to other costs of fishing and fishing tackle, line is relatively inexpensive (especially when you buy it in bulk spools). But if you happen to lose a good fish because of a bad line, you'll also realize that line can be a costly item.

The amount of line on a spool is also an indication of when to make a change. Spinning spools should be filled to about one-eighth of an inch of the lip. As you cut off sections of line because of fraying or lose line through normal fishing, casting becomes more difficult and you begin to compromise both ease and distance. You also have to run the risk of not having enough line on the spool to fight a heavy fish if it makes a long run. That's another reason for insuring that you have all your spools filled to capacity with new line.

Some anglers wait all year for their vacation and then journey to an exotic location where the brochures promise superb fishing. But these same sportsmen who dream and talk about the trip for eleven months and spend considerable money to enjoy it, will try to save a few pennies by getting by with old lines on their reels. Make it a rule to change lines on all your reels before you go on any major trip.

The other criterion for changing lines is based on subjective judgment. You must learn to evaluate how hard the line was used and what happened on the last day you spent fishing. If the line became abraded or if you have the feeling that it took quite a beating, don't gamble on the old line.

Deterioration and Shelf Life

The nylon used in monofilament line is tough material and can withstand a reasonable amount of abuse. It is affected, however, by heat and the ultraviolet rays from the sun or fluorescent lights. Generally, ultraviolet rays damage only the surface layers of line if the line is wound tightly on a storage spool or on a reel spool, making these layers weak and brittle. If the line has been in the sun for a period of time, use the series of tests outlined earlier to check it.

Nylon melts at temperatures above 500° F, but it can be damaged and weakened at lower temperatures. Temperatures below 120° F will not produce permanent damage to the monofilament, and you can usually count on considerable leeway above this. Although it is not the best policy, you can keep a reel loaded with line in the trunk of your car on a hot summer day and *probably* not affect the line. However, if you store the reel under the rear window of the automobile where both heat and the ultraviolet rays of the sun reach the line, it might require changing.

Tests have been run to determine the amount of heat generated by the friction of the line passing over the guides in the rod. Simulating the initial run of a fish by running a dry line over the guides, researchers measured temperatures up to 138° F. By seesawing the line back and forth over the same guide, temperatures have been recorded at almost 200° F—still a safe margin from the melting point of nylon at 500° F.

When lubricating a reel that has line on the spool, care should be taken to avoid getting oil or demoisturizing spray on the line. A little oil or spray might not have an adverse effect, but repeated treatments could make the line brittle or wiry, drawing out certain additives in the line.

Monofilaments are made in different colors. After repeated use, the color could begin to fade, but this in itself does not mean the line has weakened. When a line starts to lose color, though, it's still a good idea to check it carefully.

Monofilament line should always be stored away from the ultraviolet rays of the sun or fluorescent lights. The amount of moisture in the storage area is also important. When monofilament is fully saturated, it contains 9% moisture. As moisture evaporates from the line, the line will become stiffer. In the winter in a warm, dry basement, for example, the line could feel particularly stiff and may contain only 1% moisture. Before you discard the line, soak it in water for twenty-four to forty-eight hours and see if it regains its limpness.

If you store a reel that has knots in the line, the strength of the knots will diminish by about 10% after the first twenty-four hours and then remain constant. This is sometimes caused by a loss of moisture, but the usual cause is that monofilament has "memory" and tends to return to its original position. That means that the knots will slip slightly. So if you're going to fish with the same outfit you used yesterday or last week, retighten all the knots by hand before you start fishing, or take the time to tie new knots.

Selecting Monofilament Line

Although they may look identical to the untrained eye, all monofilament lines are not the same. Nylon monofilament is a compromise in the sense that, within restrictions dictated by the raw materials, manufacturers attempt to achieve a balance of properties. Every monofilament line has some degree of line strength, knot strength, stretch, limpness, shock or impact resistance, and abrasion resistance. The trick is to achieve the balance that is best suited for fishing purposes. A manufacturer can take one or two of these properties and increase them to the extremes. But in the process, he loses some of the other properties. That means that the best fishing lines have the best balance of properties.

The easiest way to choose a fishing line with the correct balance of properties is to place your confidence in a reputable manufacturer. Like anything else, you get what you pay for. There are no "good deal" or bargain lines. If a line seems relatively inexpensive, there is a reason. Usually you pay a premium for high quality control and uniformity throughout the line. If you were to run a micrometer over inexpensive line, you'd be amazed at the variations in diameter. As the diameter dips, the line strength is correspondingly weakened and the price could be that fish you wanted to land.

The line you select should be matched to the type of tackle you are using and the fishing conditions you expect to encounter. If the line is too heavy, it will prove unsporting, inhibit your casting ability, and cause knots that are too bulky. A heavy line on a light outfit just won't work and a light line on a heavy outfit will cause all kinds of problems. Within given tolerances, the breaking strength of the line should correspond to the type of tackle you prefer.

As your fishing skill increases, you can use lighter lines in the same situation, but if you are new to the game, use a slightly heavier line until you gain experience and confidence. If you're casting for trout with artificial lures, lines testing two to six pounds will fit practically any situation. The bait fisherman for trout who may have to get out of an occasional snag would do better with six- to ten-pound test line. If you're fishing for largemouth bass in relatively snag-free waters, six- to ten-pound test might prove adequate. But if you're trying to wrestle those same lunker largemouths out of a brush-lined shore or lily-pad-covered water, you may have to use lines testing over twenty pounds. That's why it makes sense to have extra spools of line for every reel you own and to load each spool with different test line. You can meet varying fishing conditions simply by changing spools.

Depending on the manufacturer, lines come in a variety of colors and shades. Some are easier for the fishermen to see and more difficult for the fish to detect. As a general rule, the color of the line is relatively unimportant in catching fish—especially when you are using a leader.

Matching Line Size to Reel Spool Diameter

Spinning enthusiasts often ignore the diameter of the spool when selecting monofilament line and merely choose the breaking strength to fit their fishing requirements. Any spinning reel designated for ultralight use should never be loaded with monofilament line above a four-pound breaking strength. Heavier line will impair casting because it will not pack properly on the spool and has a tendency to balloon off incorrectly.

Reel spools with a diameter of two inches or less should never be used with lines testing above ten pounds. The same reasoning applies. Heavier monofilament also has a greater memory factor: when it is packed in tight coils, it will retain the small coils during the cast.

At the other extreme, no mattter how large a spinning reel might be and no matter what the literature on the reels proclaim, you'll find that casting will be impaired when you use lines testing over twenty pounds. If you decide to use a line testing more than twenty pounds on spinning tackle, you should be aware of the shortcomings.

Some reels include an extra spool of smaller capacity for those fishing situations where you won't need as much line. When fishing light lines or at those times when a fish could run a considerable distance, don't make the mistake of not using a spool with enough line capacity to counter any move by the fish. And whenever you refill a spool of line, it pays to discard the whole line and put on a full spool of new line. You might get by with merely changing the first hundred yards, but it could eventually catch up with you.

Limpness versus Stiffness

Somewhere along the historical road of spinning, someone decided that limpness was important for casting and that a spinning line should be ultralimp. This error has persisted through the years and limp monofilament is made and advertised because a surprising number of fishermen still believe that they should use it. Limpness is defined technically as the amount of force required to bend or deflect a line.

When you examine the subject closely, monofilament was tailored for spinning use because braided line proved to be *too* limp. Without some degree of stiffness, line will not balloon off the spool properly when you cast. Contrary to popular opinion, repeated tests have shown that an ultralimp line will not cast as well as a medium limp (or medium stiff) line under most conditions because it won't balloon off the spool correctly. At the other end of the spectrum, a very stiff line will snarl during the cast and create additional problems.

For the majority of fishing situations, your best choice would be a medium stiff line. The only exception is for an ultralight reel in line tests under four pounds where the limp line will exhibit less memory factor and spool more easily in the tight coils necessary. Keep in mind, however, that limp line has more stretch than a medium stiff line, knots slip in it more easily, and it is more difficult to set the hook with limp line.

You'll find that the best fishermen in the country ignore ultralimp lines and demonstrate a specific preference for those monofilaments that are medium stiff (or medium limp).

Unknotted Line Strength

Unknotted line strength can be defined as the break load of the line without any knots in it divided by the diameter of the line. It is really a measurement of tensile strength. A more practical definition for fishing purposes would be the breaking strength of the line expressed in pounds such as ten-pound test, twelve-pound test, and so forth. Within reasonable tolerances, manufacturers try to reduce the diameter of the line while holding the breaking strength constant. If the diameter is smaller for a given strength, you can get more line on the reel, experience less wind resistance when you cast, less friction in the water, and the line will lie more evenly on the spool in tightly packed coils.

It's important to realize that monofilament line has uniform strength throughout. Some anglers believe that most of the strength is concentrated in what they call the outer shell of the line, but this is not true. If you were to shave 10% of the surface area from ten-pound test line, you would have nine-pound test line.

Another thing to keep in mind is that you can change the shape of the line without affecting the breaking strength. This happens most frequently when you tie a knot and then notice that the section of line adjacent to the knot has been flattened out. All you've really done is rearrange the nylon, but the strength will stay the same unless you've nicked the line in the process.

A sharp nick in monofilament is another matter. It is not the same as shaving the line uniformly. Instead, a nick causes what researchers refer to as a stress concentration and greatly weakens the line. In computing the effect of a stress concentration, the breaking factor is multiplied by two or three so that ten-pound test line may break at six pounds at the point of the nick. To better understand the effects of a stress concentration, try to tear a polyethylene bag in half. The plastic, just like monofilament, is tough. But if you take a sharp object and put a small nick in the bag, you can rip it easily. That's why any line that has been nicked should be changed immediately.

Fishermen sometimes discover that one brand of monofilament is stronger than another even though both are rated at the same breaking strength. They are basing their observations on the stated breaking strength that appears on the labels and that's where the fallacy lies. Labeling laws in the United States dictate that the label must accurately reflect the product. If a label on a spool of line states that the line is ten-pound test, the line cannot legally break *under* ten-pound test. That leaves the final decision as to the actual breaking strength with the manufacturer. If he chooses, he can take a spool of line that breaks at fifteen-pound test and label it ten-pound test, and he is completely within the law. So, when one line seems stronger than another, it probably is; but you may be using a line that is much stronger than the breaking strength indicated on the label.

The only exception to this occurs with lines manufactured for tournament participation. In that case, the label guarantees that the line will not break over a specified strength. Thirty-pound test tournament rated line, for example, is guaranteed to break below thirty pounds of straight pull.

Repeated loading and unloading of a monofilament line—that is, applying tension and then removing it (such as you might expect when fighting a fish) —does not weaken a line as long as this tension is below the breaking strength. But if you do approach the breaking strength repeatedly, you could conceivably weaken the line.

Impact Resistance Compared to Line Strength

If you want to break a piece of light line in your hands, you would normally let a small belly or U form in the line between your two hands and then snap your hands apart. Experience tells you that it is easier to break line this way than to exert a steady pressure on a tight line. What you have done (and probably unknowingly) is to load the line quickly under stress, which affects its ability to withstand impact rather than its normal breaking strength.

Impact or shock resistance is the ability of a line to withstand a sudden shock. Line strength is measured with a steady pull and is a static test. The impact factor varies with the length of line and the rate at which it is loaded.

Let's go back to the example of breaking line in your hands. The faster you snap your hands apart, the easier it is to break the line. Try it! If you pull your hands apart slowly, you probably won't break the line. The second aspect of impact resistance is the length of line over which this shock is distributed. The longer the length of line, the more area for the shock to be absorbed. This same factor will also break knots. That's why it is always important to exert steady pressure while fighting a fish. If you persist in jerking the rod, you are dealing with impact strength and that can be a lot weaker than normal breaking strength.

One of the compensating factors that reduces impact is the amount of stretch in the line. Your fishing rod also helps to cushion the effect. But it is well to remember that, under most circumstances, a line should be kept tight while playing a fish. If the line were to come tight suddenly, the breaking strength of the line would be replaced temporarily by impact strength and the effect would be the same as snapping the line apart in your hands.

On the other hand, fish seldom produce impact of any significance. You might think they do, but researchers using delicate instruments have measured every aspect from the strike to the net and found that it just doesn't happen unless you permit a fish to surge against a loose line and a tight drag. So, impact is a problem that plagues inexperienced anglers because they are likely to work the rod in a jerky motion or allow slack to form and then tighten it up suddenly.

Impact resistance is another argument in favor of selecting fishing lines that are manufactured under rigid quality-control conditions. When diameter varies, line strength also varies and so does impact strength. All you need in a line is a small section of smaller diameter and strength and it just might not withstand a sudden shock.

Knot Strength

Knot strength is a measure of the breaking strength of a line that has been knotted. It is usually expressed as a percentage of the unknotted line strength since most knots weaken the line. Thus, the knots invariably become the weakest link in the chain between you and the fish. There are a few knots, however, that are rated at 100% of the unknotted line strength and they should be used whenever possible. Some people believe that the 100% knots are stronger than the unknotted line, but researchers point out that this is not true. The reason this fallacious thinking developed is that, when the line is subjected to pressures that exceed the breaking strength, the line breaks while the knot remains. That does not mean that the knot is stronger than the line. Once you tie a 100% knot, whether the line breaks in the standing part or in the knot is dictated by chance alone. Although monofilament is very uniform, it is not absolutely uniform and will break at the point of least diameter, which could be as slight as 1/10,000 of an inch. If the point of least diameter occurs in the knot (by chance alone), the knot will break. Otherwise the line will break.

Some knots will tax the capability of a line more than others, while some types of monofilament are basically better for tying knots. The veteran angler can tie a good knot in almost any line, but the average fisherman generally is careless about knots, making the property of knot strength even more critical.

As a general rule, an exceptionally limp line has poor knot strength. The reason is that the line is soft and it compresses like a pillow when pressure is exerted. Once you get slippage or compression in a knot, the knot will collapse. The weakest knot you can tie is the overhand knot because one strand cuts through the other under pressure. Any deficiency in the line will show up fastest if you tie an overhand knot and try to break the line. But an overhand knot is also the ideal way to test the knot strength in a line. It will measure the vulnerability of a line to poor knots and, if a line can demonstrate strength with the overhand knot, other knots should reach their maximum strength.

In some lines, an overhand knot will break at 40% to 50% of the unknotted line strength. However, those lines with good knot strength hold an overhand knot up to 75% of the unknotted line strength.

Abrasion Resistance

Abrasion resistance or the ability to resist scuffing and nicking is an inherent property of a particular material. Either the material has it or it doesn't. Nylon is tough and abrasion resistant; and the hardness or stiffness of the mono has little to do with it. There are some anglers who continue to believe that the stiff or "hard" type of monofilament is more abrasion resistant than limp or "soft" monofilament, but filament specialists tell us that this is another common misconception.

Although the abrasion-resistant qualities of both stiff and limp monofilament are basically the same, limp or soft mono will resist abrasion better than the stiff or hard type, but for another reason. Soft monofilament has a tendency to "give" and will move away from a hard object. It's like trying to slice a rubber band with a knife. The rubber band will move away from the knife blade because it's soft, flexible, and elastic.

If you intend to land fish consistently, you must be alert to abrasion in monofilament. Fish with sharp teeth or gill covers can rough up a line or leader quickly. If your quarry drags the line over the bottom, you can bet that it will become abraded and the damaged section should be removed as soon as the fish is landed. But most abrasion occurs from guides on rods that are nicked or grooved and from rollers on spinning reels that fail to turn under pressure. This is a much more common occurrence than most anglers suspect. If you have any doubts, watch the roller the next time a fish is taking line. And if you're still not sure, take a felt-tip marker and put a line across the roller. If that line remains stationary, your roller isn't turning. You'll also find that guides and rollers made from tungsten carbide are hard on monofilament line and have a tendency to abrade the line faster than guides and rollers made from other materials.

Stretch, the Magic Ingredient

Anyone who has used monofilament line is aware of its tendency to stretch when a load is applied. If you happen to hook bottom or plant your lure in a streamside bush and try to pull it loose, you can actually see and feel the amount of stretch. The limper the monofilament, the more stretch it has. The stiffer the monofilament, the less stretch it has. Think of it in terms of wire versus a rubber band and the stretch property should become apparent.

The critical aspect is that the amount of stretch must be controlled. We talked earlier about a balance of properties, and stretch is directly tied into the degree of limpness and the impact strength. A reasonable amount of stretch in monofilament makes the line "forgiving." You can make a mistake in fighting the fish or setting the hook and still get away with it because the stretch in the line will help to compensate for your error. On the other hand, you can't set the hook with a rubber band, and too much stretch will make the line unfishable. If a line has too much stretch, you won't be able to pump a fish toward you and casting will be impaired because the line won't balloon off the spool properly. If there's too little stretch, impact resistance goes way down and a sudden surge by the fish could break the line. Stretch helps to decelerate and reduce the impact. It's as if you drove a car into a brick wall as compared to a haystack. You'll stop in either case, but the brick wall will stop the car suddenly, while the haystack will slow it down first.

In knot tying, a line with too much stretch makes it difficult to draw a knot tight. Instead of being properly seated, the knot could be holding by only one or two strands and knot strength will be substantially reduced. Thus, the best monofilament for tying knots is a medium stiff line that exhibits a balance of properties that includes controlled stretch.

The Effects of Moisture

Nylon is directly affected by the amount of moisture in the air and it has the property of absorbing this moisture from the air if the relative humidity is high enough. When you fish, a line picks up moisture from both the air and water, so that at the end of a day's fishing it could be pretty well saturated. A fully saturated monofilament line contains about 9% water. This might not seem significant until you realize that there is a marked difference between the breaking strength of the line when it is dry compared to when it is wet.

Fully saturated monofilament is approximately 15% weaker than dry line. Line is usually rated for label purposes on the basis of its wet strength. And when monofilament loses its water content, it becomes stiffer. Since you can never tell how much water the line holds at any given moment, you can never be exactly certain of its breaking strength at a specific period in time unless the line is fully saturated.

The water absorption rate depends on the diameter of the line and the length of time it is immersed. Generally, it takes from twenty-four to forty-eight hours to saturate a perfectly dry line. Water absorption and loss also varies with the type of reel you are using. A closed-face spinning reel has the tendency to retain moisture, which is then absorbed by the line. The reason is that the spool of line has little contact with the air except through a couple of small openings.

The same thing happens when you store a reel that has just been fished in a tackle box or reel case. On the other hand, moisture is often trapped in an open-faced reel under the coils of line. It will evaporate from the top layers, but the tightly packed coils beneath will trap the water until the line absorbs it. So, the next time you fish with the reel, you might find that the first several feet of line are slightly stiffer than the rest of the line. This, of course, has been caused by evaporation of water in the line.

Although many tournaments and record-keeping organizations announce that they perform wet tests on the lines submitted, many erroneously believe that two hours submersion is all that is necessary. Two hours submersion creates a state of nonequilibrium and although a certain amount of water absorption has taken place, the line is not at its correct wet strength in the majority of cases. If you must submit a line for testing, the best procedure is to soak it for twenty-four hours, seal the line in a plastic bag with a few drops of water inside the bag, and ship it off to the testing facility. The line will absorb the few drops of water in the bag and will appear dry when it arrives—and you'll get a fair wet test.

Buying Line

Monofilament fishing line comes packaged in a variety of ways. For some spinning reels, you can buy extra spools that are already prewound with line of a stated breaking strength. You also have the option of buying interconnected spools or bulk spools. Bulk spools are generally designated by weight—that is, quarter-pound, half-pound, and one-pound spools. How much line you get on a particular spool depends on the breaking strength and the diameter of the line.

Fishermen are seldom as careful in shopping for line as they are for other items of tackle. They'll take all kinds of time to select a rod or reel, but simply walk up to a tackle dealer and ask for ten-pound test line. If you intend to spool your own line, it makes sense to buy it in at least quarter-pound spools. One reason is that you can put on the exact amount that the reel requires instead of being limited to hundred yard increments. You'll also find that top-rated fishermen refuse to spool line from interconnected spools. Their reasoning is that there could be a nick, abrasion, or worn spot where the spools interconnect and they are not about to take a chance.

If you prefer to have your tackle dealer spool the line for you, he will almost always take it off a bulk spool. Since monofilament can deteriorate, it is best to ask to check the spool before the line is put on the reel. Go through the tests outlined to determine if the line is usable. Who knows, he may have kept it near a front window where sun and heat damaged it.

There are a number of line winders on the market that can make spooling on new line a much easier task. Some are simple plastic devices that hold bulk spools up to a quarter pound, while others are motor driven and are only necessary if you spool a lot of line. There are also some basic line winders that clamp to your workbench and operate by turning the handle manually. Any of these is a worthwhile investment and you can buy some of the less expensive ones for under five dollars. Or, if you are handy with tools, you can build your own.

Removing old line from a spool can be done in a variety of ways. You can use line winders to crank it off on an empty bulk spool, and some of the electric line winders have specially shaped cones for that purpose. If you haven't any of these conveniences, you can rig up an empty bulk spool on a quarter-inch drill by pushing a bolt through the spool and into the chuck on the drill. As the drill revolves, it will remove the line for you.

Loading Line on a Reel

If you are using interconnected spools, the first step is either to tape the spools together or slip a rubber band through the center hole in each spool and lock the rubber band in place by placing a small nail through the rubber band loop on the outside of the end spools. This will insure that the spools will turn together when you are spooling line on the reel.

When spooling line on a revolving spool or conventional reel, put a pencil through the spool or spools of new line. Have someone hold both ends of the pencil and simply crank the new line on the reel. Don't let the line balloon off the end of the bulk spool. That will put twist in the line.

Problems in spooling line can occur with spinning reels because the reel spool is stationary and the rotating head and bail wind the line around the spool. If you use a loading machine in which the reel spool is removed and attached to the machine, the line will be put on without twist. Few fishermen realize, however, that when you cast and the line balloons off the reel spool, you are putting one twist in the line for every coil. As you retrieve, the twist is forced toward the lure and automatically removed from the line. Thus, when you lift the lure from the water, you often see it spinning. That removes the last of the twist before the next cast, so that no problems of twist are caused.

With spinning reels, another method of loading line is to let the new line balloon off the service spool. Since twist is additive, the line must come off the service spool in the same direction it goes on the reel spool. Consider that there is a Side A and Side B to every service spool. If you place the spool on one side plate, the line comes off in one direction. Turn the spool over on the other side plate and the coils will reverse direction. By pointing the reel directly at the bulk spool, you can quickly tell if the bail is turning the same way the line is coming off. This will negate any line twist.

Even for spinning reels, the best method is to put a pencil through the bulk service spool and merely crank the line on the reel. In this case, you'll be putting one twist in the line for every revolution of the reel. Each time you cast, this twist will come out via the coils ballooning off the reel and the line will lie on the water without any twist. As you retrieve the line, the one twist comes back, only to be negated again on the next cast.

As you spool line on any reel, clamp it between your thumb and forefinger to apply a little bit of tension. This will help to pack the line tightly and evenly on the spool. It doesn't take much pressure to do this, but if you don't pack the line on evenly and tightly, strands could become buried when a fish takes line against the drag.

Spinning spools should be filled to within one-eighth of an inch of the lip. If you overfill a spinning spool, the first or second cast will result in a tangle and you'll have to cut the excess line off anyway. In filling a conventional reel, consider whether or not the reel has a level-wind mechanism that will spool line evenly. If it doesn't, allow a greater margin of safety between the spooled line and the reel pillars. When fighting a fish, it is sometimes difficult to spool the line back on evenly and you could experience a line buildup on one side. If you don't leave room for this, you won't be able to turn the handle of the reel because the line will jam against the pillars and you'll either have to hand-line your fish or try to straighten out the mess with a fish on the other end.

A few fly-reel manufacturers include literature with their reels telling you how much backing of a given test the reel will hold plus a fly line of a specified size and taper. In the absence of this information, or to be perfectly certain, you'll have to employ another method. The trick is to start with the fly line and wind it on the reel first. Then fill the balance of the reel with backing. When the reel is full, strip off the backing and fly line and reverse the procedure so the backing goes on first. And if you want to get more backing on the reel, you can cut off part of the running line on a weight-forward fly line. The fly line will be shorter, but you'll still have plenty to cast with. You'll gain on the backing because more yards of backing can fill the space previously occupied by the fly line.

Expansion of Monofilament under Pressure

Monofilament line has a property that scientists refer to as memory. This is nothing more than the tendency of the line to return to its original position after it has been stretched or stored in a certain way. Memory is clearly evident when you squeeze a sponge. The moment you release the pressure, the sponge returns to its original shape.

Because of memory, monofilament can sometimes generate a tremendous force in its attempt to return to the original position. This force can actually explode a reel spool and twist the spool completely out of shape. It occurs when an angler packs monofilament too tightly on the spool. This seldom happens while loading line, but it could occur when playing a fish. The pressure of the fish on one end of the line sometimes packs the coils on the reel too tightly. If you've just been through a hectic battle with a fish, strip one hundred yards or so of the mono off your reel and into the water. Then reel it back under normal tension. Spools don't explode very often, but this precaution could help to save one for you.

That's also the reason that backing for fly reels should be braided Dacron instead of monofilament. Dacron doesn't expand or stretch as much as monofilament does and it lacks the memory so that it won't explode the narrow fly-reel spool.

It's worth another reminder at this point that you should always apply a little tension whenever you spool monofilament on a reel, regardless of the circumstances. The cake of monofilament must be packed tightly so that one strand won't bury itself under pressure. When you reel in a line that is on the water, surface tension of the water helps to apply the slight pressure for you. You'll also discover that lighter lines form a much more even cake than heavier mono and there is less tendency for them to bury.

Line Twist

Monofilament line can become twisted in a number of ways, including the method you use to spool it on the reel. The two most common causes of line twist are the failure to use a swivel (or using inefficient swivels) and, on spinning reels, turning the handle of the reel without regaining line.

Anglers have a tendency to cut corners when it comes to buying swivels and they will often settle for less than the best even though swivels are very inexpensive. Some lures such as weighted spinners, spoons, and even certain plugs are much more prone to twist than other lures. And don't discount the fact that natural bait often twists in a current or when you are reeling it in. The answer lies in top-quality swivels, bead chain, and even swivels with ball bearings. If the swivel doesn't absorb the twist, you can bet that the line will.

Spinning tackle is the most popular type of fishing tackle in use today and, because of its simplicity of operation, it is the choice of millions of newcomers to fishing. When a fish is hooked, neophyte anglers become excited and tend to forget what they have learned. The result is that the spinning reel becomes a winch and the angler continues cranking and cranking the handle even though the drag is slipping and the reel is not gaining any line. Most spinning reels have a retrieve ratio that surpasses three to one. For every full revolution of the handle, the bail has rotated at least three times. Every time the bail on the spinning reel makes one revolution without spooling line, one twist is put in the line at the spool. Since twist is additive, with modern retrieve ratios it doesn't take long to create a tangled mess of twisted line.

If a line isn't twisted too badly, the twist can be removed by cutting off all terminal tackle, including swivels, and trolling the line behind a moving boat. But in cases where the twist is bad, the only alternative is to replace the line and try to remember next time that you must pump a fish toward you and only turn the handle of the reel when line can be recovered.

Although it cannot be considered line twist in the true sense of the word, leader material removed from a coil exhibits memory common to monofilament and tends to remain in a coiled condition. Naturally, leader material should be straight and there are a couple of ways to solve the problem. The first is simply to tie the end to something or have someone hold it and pull steadily. With heavy mono leader, you can usually pull the kinks out.

A better method is to use heat—either through friction or by immersing the coils of leader material in warm water. Friction can be created by pulling the leader material through a small piece of leather or rubber that has been doubled over. You can even use your fingers, though this could cause a line burn. In an emergency, leader material can be pulled under a boot or shoe, but if you're in waders or rubber boots, make sure the line doesn't cut through the rubber.

Choosing Leader Material

Originally, most knowledgeable anglers preferred stiff or hard nylon monofilament leader material because they believed it was more abrasion resistant. That has changed now. As a general rule, you should always select the lightest leader material dictated by the situation and your own experience. In salt water for some species, this might be sixty- or eighty-pound test, or, if the fish don't have sharp teeth, it might be as low as twenty-pound test.

Anglers sometimes have a tendency to skimp on the use of leader material. The best way to buy the heavier leader material is in quarter-pound spools. When you tie knots, cut off more material than you will need and then trim off the excess when you have completed the knot. It's a cheap investment, and knot tying is a lot easier if you don't have to struggle with short ends.

Some of us have now switched to limp or medium stiff monofilament for the butt sections of fly leaders because we find they perform much better than the stiffer material. The tippets of the fly leaders are made from medium stiff or stiff monofilament to help turn the fly over.

3 OTHER LINES AND LEADERS

Braided Lines

Since the days of the old "squidding" lines, braided lines have been improved considerably; today most of them are made from Dacron. A braided line (as the name implies) is made from twisting or braiding fibers of Dacron or nylon. Originally, braided lines were made from linen, silk, and similar materials. Monofilament, on the other hand, is a single filament that is extruded and then oriented.

Of all braided lines, Dacron is the most popular. It has very little stretch when compared to nylon monofilament, and for that reason it is a very "unforgiving" line—unforgiving in the sense that if you make a mistake or error in judgment when applying pressure to the line, it will break. There isn't a cushion (stretch) to absorb the shock. Because of the lack of stretch (which approximates 10% in Dacron compared to 30% in monofilament), it is much easier to set the hook with Dacron. But if you apply just a bit too much pressure on the strike, you'll break the line. It can be that critical.

In deep jigging or any situation in which the angler is trying to impart action to a lure such as a lead-headed bucktail, the lack of stretch in Dacron can cancel out some of the action of the lure. Deep-fished bucktails work better with nylon monofilament where the stretch in the line and the memory of the line (the tendency to return to its original position) help to provide the proper action. On the other hand, Dacron is not affected by the ultraviolet rays of light and it maintains relatively the same strength wet or dry.

Some freshwater fishermen still prefer Dacron line for bait casting (called plug casting in salt water), but the majority of anglers using this type of tackle now favor monofilament. One problem is that a revolving spool reel is prone to backlash, and Dacron can be radically weakened if it is pinched or frayed in a backlash. Dacron also has lower knot strength than monofilament and it requires the use of a few selected knots. Knots for monofilament don't hold well in Dacron.

Braided Dacron has two other major uses. It is the primary choice of fly fishermen for backing on their fly reels because it does not stretch under pressure and then return to its original position as monofilament does. This stretching and subsequent contraction of monofilament can spring or explode reel spools.

In addition, braided Dacron is often used on conventional saltwater trolling tackle in the eighty- and one-hundred-thirty-pound classes. The main reason for this is that Dacron has less stretch. With big game tackle and a heavy fish on the end, the angler must work hard. Using monofilament, he would be fighting the tackle and the stretch in the line as much as the fish. This would cause him to work much harder than he would have to with Dacron. It would also be hard to set a hook over a considerable distance with monofilament. With billfish and a normal dropback, there can be a substantial number of yards between angler and fish when the hook is set.

Another argument given for the use of Dacron on heavy trolling tackle is that monofilament in the larger sizes has a greater diameter than Dacron of the same breaking strength. That means that an angler can spool more Dacron on the same reel than he could monofilament. However, this argument has become somewhat nebulous of late as monofilament manufacturers have become more successful in reducing diameter while holding the breaking strength constant.

Wire Leaders

Before discussing wire leaders, it should be pointed out that seasoned anglers will always use monofilament leaders in preference to wire whenever they feel that wire is not absolutely necessary. Experience has demonstrated that even though monofilament has a larger diameter than wire, it will still bring more strikes. Fish often exhibit a shyness to wire. Monofilament is also more supple and will sometimes produce a better action with a lure or bait. And it does not kink or twist as wire does. So, if you can get by with monofilament, use it instead of wire.

There are three types of wire leaders currently in use in both fresh- and saltwater fishing situations. The most popular type is single-strand stainless-steel wire that is used as protection against sharp teeth, razor-edged gill covers, and bills on the larger billfish. Sailfish enthusiasts now prefer mono leaders of hundred-pound test to wire. Your choice should be based on whether or not a fish can cut through monofilament. If it can, use wire. Wire, of course, is almost invariably the choice for rigging natural trolling baits.

Single-strand wire is sized or gauged by a series of numbers starting at #2 and running through #19. The same system applies to stainless-steel wire in silver or coffee color; most anglers, by the way, prefer coffee color. The lower the number, the lighter the breaking strength of the wire. As an example, #2 wire from one manufacturer is .011 inches in diameter and will break at twenty-eight pounds. For each .001 inches between #2 and #5 wire, the gauge or size is increased by one. Number 4 wire from this fabricator would be .013 inches in diameter. Above #5 wire, each size is .002 inches more in diameter than the preceding size. This, of course, might vary with the manufacturer, but each maker will follow a similar pattern.

Single-strand wire is excellent for rigging trolling baits and it can be connected easily with the Haywire Twist. The one drawback is that, if the wire should kink, you cannot straighten it without weakening the wire. And if it does kink, it could break that quickly. It also offers the least diameter compared to the breaking strength of any type of wire.

Some fishermen prefer to use braided wire leaders because they are more supple and will not kink (although they *can* curl). Braided wire—like braided line—has several strands twisted together. It is available plain or with a plastic (nylon) coating over the wire. This becomes a question of choice and both types enjoy some degree of popularity. When measured against single-strand wire, braided wire is slightly larger in diameter for the same breaking strength and nylon-coated wire is considerably larger than either of the other two types.

Braided wire is sized by breaking strength (there are no gauge numbers) and you simply buy twenty-seven-pound test, forty-pound test, or any other strength you want. Single-strand wire comes in coils of so many feet or by weight in quarter-pound, half-pound, and one-pound coils. Braided wire is generally spooled and you buy so many feet or you can buy it in bulk by weight.

Aircraft Cable

Aircraft cable is used solely as leader material for big game fishing for marlin, sharks, and a few other heavyweight species. It is fabricated from as many as forty-nine strands of wire that have been braided or twisted together, offering the advantages of flexibility and kink resistance. With a marlin, for example, when the fish jumps, it could easily kink or twist single-strand wire. Aircraft cable can take a great deal of abuse and is the ideal choice for this type of fishing.

When you run your hands over aircraft cable, it is relatively smooth, but during the course of battle with a big fish, it is possible to create a few burrs on the cable. For this reason, whenever aircraft cable is handled with a fish on the end, the cockpit crew should wear heavy gloves or at least two pairs of cotton gloves.

Lead-core and Solid-wire Lines

Lead-core and solid-wire lines are basically in the province of trolling enthusiasts who sometimes must get baits and lures deeper than usual to present an offering at fish-eye level. A typical example is the lake-trout angler who has relied on copper or bronze line for many, many years during the summer months when it becomes necessary to drag a bait through the lower reaches of a deep lake. On the saltwater scene, there are equally valid reasons for employing wire line. Lines made from stainless steel or Monel wire are better suited for ocean work because they won't rust. It is important to note, however, that some tournaments, contests, and record-keeping organizations specifically disallow wire line of any type.

Wire lines are relatively soft and come in a variety of breaking strengths, although the majority in use test between eighteen and forty-five pounds. The greatest problem in wire lines is that they kink easily—which can cause the line to break. They are not as strong as they may look. It's therefore incumbent upon the user to exercise extreme caution when spooling or letting out the wire. The click mechanism on the reel should always be engaged when setting the baits or lures astern to prevent the wire from free-spooling and tangling; and it doesn't hurt to use your thumb on the reel spool to help pay out line slowly and smoothly.

When recovering wire line, you must make certain it is spooled evenly on the reel. Otherwise, it will build up in a pile and then tumble off under the reel pillars, causing an almost unbelievable tangle. For that reason, reel manufacturers recommend certain narrow spool models for use with wire. However, some anglers prefer wider spool reels, reasoning that it is easier to remove a backlash if it occurs when there is more room on the spool. Wire is used only with conventional reels.

It is not necessary to fill an entire reel with wire line. Instead, most anglers will use from fifty to a hundred yards of wire attached to Dacron backing. Experience is the best guide in determining how much line must be let out at a given trolling speed to reach the desired depth. Veterans mark the wire with tape or nail polish at regular intervals so that they can tell at a glance how much wire is streaming astern.

Instead of solid wire, some fishermen prefer to use lead-core line. Lead core has a solid strand of wire running through the middle, but it is then coated with a braiding. You won't experience the same kinking problems with lead core as you will with solid wire because the braid adds flexibility; but you must be careful not to bend the lead core too severely or you could break the solid core inside.

Lead core does not sink as fast as solid wire because of the increased diameter. Another little-known fact is that, regardless of rated breaking strength, lead core has the same amount of wire inside. The difference in breaking strength is gained through the amount of braid over the wire. This means that the lighter tests will sink faster because of the same weight matched against a smaller diameter.

Fly fishermen have been using thirty feet of lead core to form a shooting head designed to gain distance while carrying the fly relatively deep. The shooting head is attached to one hundred feet of monofilament running line (or level fly line) and then to braided Dacron.

Fly Lines

Back in the days of Izaak Walton, fly lines were made from braided horsehair. Later, line makers started to mix silk with horsehair, and finally they went to an all-silk fly line. Today, fly lines are manufactured from heat-cured plastic finishes applied over a level core of nylon or Dacron, allowing the maker rigid control of diameter and weight. Tapers are created in the coating, and specific gravity can be controlled, insuring that a line will either float or sink. A few manufacturers are now marketing fly lines made on a monofilament base. These lines require special knots for connecting backing or leaders.

Basically, there are two types of fly lines—those that float and those that sink. Floating fly lines are preferred in the multitude of fishing situations and they are certainly recommended for the beginner because of the ease with which they can be lifted off the water. Sinking fly lines have special applications where the angler wants to fish a fly well below the surface or get a fly down quickly in a fast stream. They are gaining in popularity for many types of fishing, and most skilled fly-rod enthusiasts carry both types of line with them.

Since it is the weight of the line that carries the fly, the distribution of this weight or the taper of the line is important. There are four primary types of tapers from which an angler can choose. The most basic is the level fly line that has uniform diameter from one end to the other. This is the lowest-priced fly line and it is extremely useful when a particularly delicate presentation is required. The double-tapered fly lines are of the same diameter through most of the length, but they taper at each end to a smaller diameter. A double-tapered fly line is an ideal line for roll casting and can also be used for delicate presentations. Another advantage is that you can reverse the line and use the other end when the first side wears out.

The majority of fly-fishermen today have switched to weight-forward fly lines. These lines have a short front taper, a heavy belly section, a short back taper, and small-diameter running line. The weight and bulk of the line is concentrated up front, permitting better casting from a standpoint of both speed of presentation and distance. They are made to "shoot" line—that is, the heavy front taper pulls the lighter line with it once the cast is made.

The fourth type of fly line is the single taper or shooting head. This is nothing more than the first thirty feet of a weight-forward fly line with a loop spliced in the back end. Monofilament running line is attached to this loop and it enables the caster to obtain greater distance. Shooting heads are usually of the sinking variety and they are favorites among West Coast steelhead fishermen.

In order to achieve uniformity among fly-line manufacturers, the American Fishing Tackle Manufacturers Association (AFTMA) has established a system of fly-line standards based on the weight of the first thirty feet of fly line. This weight is expressed in terms of a number system from 1 to 12 which reflects the number of grains (437.5 = 1 ounce) in the first thirty feet. The following table reflects the weight of each line size:

Line Number	Weight (*In Grains*)	Tolerance Range (*In Grains*)
1	60	54–60
2	80	74–86
3	100	94–106
4	120	114–126
5	140	134–146
6	160	152–168
7	185	177–193
8	210	202–218
9	240	230–250
10	280	270–290
11	330	318–342
12	380	368–392

The beauty of this system is that regardless of the type of line you select or the taper, if it is a #6 line, it should weigh 160 grains. So, once you determine the weight line for a particular rod, you can replace it easily or add additional lines to your inventory on the number system alone. However, we would be remiss if we did not point out that although this system works in theory, there are sometimes broader tolerances in practice. You might find, for example, that a #8 line from one manufacturer corresponds to a #7 line from another.

The AFTMA has also developed a code to identify the various lines. A level fly line is identified by the letter (L), double taper (DT), weight forward (WF), and single taper (ST). If the line floats, it is marked with the letter (F), and if it sinks, with an (S). There are a few lines that sink very, very slowly and they are known as intermediate lines. These are designated by the letter (I).

The prefix letter denotes the type of fly line, while the suffix letter tells whether the line floats or sinks. The number in the middle corresponds to the weight standards. Thus, a WF-8-F fly line is a weight-forward floater of approximately 210 grains. A DT-5-S would be a double-taper sinking fly line of about 140 grains.

The key to successful fly-fishing is in balancing the fly line to the fly rod. When the system is in balance, casting is much easier and certainly more effortless. Most recommendations on this subject suggest to the angler that he buy the rod and then match the correct weight line to that particular rod. We prefer to look at the problem differently. Our belief is that you must first determine the size flies you will be casting for the fish you want to catch. Then, select the fly line that can handle flies of that size. And then, buy a rod that will be the perfect mate for the fly line you have selected. A heavier fly line can obviously carry light flies, but a light line will collapse if subjected to the weight and wind resistance of heavier flies. Eventually, every fly-fisherman will have more than one outfit in his arsenal, but each one should still be selected for a particular job.

4 KNOTS YOU SHOULD KNOW

THOUGH there are hundreds of different knots in use by fishermen today, a fair percentage are less than effective. The reason is that few anglers assign the degree of importance to knot tying that it merits. Not many fishermen have learned to recognize the difference between knot failure and line failure. As far as they are concerned, a broken line is a broken line—even if that break occurs in the knot.

On the other hand, a number of knots appear to be relatively strong because the average angler does not put his tackle to the maximum test in fighting a fish. In this chapter, we have attempted to select those knots that have been tested extensively, ignoring a multitude of additional ties. The knots used by the top fishermen in the world are here. The secret of knot tying is not how many knots you know how to tie, but which ones you can tie well. Leading anglers invariably limit themselves to less than a dozen knots. They may be able to tie many more, but they restrict their fishing knots to those that have been proven in practice; and they are reluctant to switch to other knots until they are firmly convinced the new knots are better.

The knots in this chapter have been carefully grouped on the basis of use. Select one or two knots in each section and learn to tie them. Then, you may want to go back and master some of the others. Remember also that not everyone will be able to tie every knot. If you find you simply cannot handle a particular knot, select another one from the same group.

You'll find that it is easier to tie a knot in lighter line, so when you are learning a knot, stick to line tests between ten and fifteen pounds. Select a time when your mental attitude includes patience and willingness to learn. It's going to take a few tries before you begin to grasp the procedure for a given knot. But, with a little practice, you'll be able to tie most knots in this book quickly, effectively, and consistently.

When you have selected a knot you want to learn, spend a few minutes reading the text and studying the illustrations. Try to comprehend the basics of the knot and what you are trying to accomplish. Then start slowly and follow each step carefully. We have written the instructions for right-handed tyers. If you are left-handed, the hand positions will be reversed.

How to Draw a Knot up Correctly

The most common failure in knot tying (and the cause of the majority of poor knots) occurs when the tyer attempts to draw the knot tight. He may have gone through the motions correctly, but he fails to seat the knot properly and it subsequently fails. Particularly in monofilament, drawing a knot up tight is paramount to success. Remember that a knot in monofilament will start to slip just before it breaks.

Before attempting to draw any knot tight, it should be lubricated with saliva from your mouth or by putting the loosely formed knot in water for a second or two. Equally important, every knot should be tightened with a *steady, continuous pull.* Once you start applying pressure to tighten the knot, don't stop until the knot is completely seated. The single greatest failing of most knot tyers is the tendency to tighten in stages with a series of pulls rather than with one steady pull.

Particularly with heavier breaking strengths, it may be necessary to wear gloves or wrap a handkerchief or cloth around your hands to prevent the line from cutting. Actually, the cutting effect of the line on your hands isn't as critical as the fact that you cannot pull heavier lines tight with bare hands. Researchers discovered, for example, that an average man with bare hands can exert only twenty pounds of pull on a knot in fifty-pound-test monofilament. Yet, to tighten that knot to only 85% efficiency requires a pull of twenty-nine pounds. The same average man can exert only twenty-seven pounds of pull on eighty-pound-test monofilament, yet 85% knot efficiency is not reached until the pull exceeds thirty-seven pounds.

When you have drawn a knot tight, exert a steady pull once or twice more to make sure the knot does not break. It is much better to have a knot break in your hands and have the opportunity to retie it than to have it break on a fish.

Finally, there is one exception to every rule and in this case it is the Blood or Barrel Knot. This is the only knot that must be tightened with a sharp jerk (in breaking strengths above six-pound test) instead of a steady pull. Otherwise the coils of line in the knot will not tighten uniformly.

How to Trim a Knot

Most knots that are seated properly can be trimmed closely, because they won't slip. Trimming can be done with a pair of nail clippers, scissors, or cutting pliers, but under no circumstances should the end of a knot be burned with a match or cigarette to remove the tag end. The heat could weaken the line in the strands of the knot and thus reduce the breaking strength.

Generally, a knot should be trimmed close to the tie so that the tag ends do not project. If they do, they could catch on a guide or in the tip-top of the rod. In cases where a tag end should be left a little longer, we will note the specific trimming instructions with the knot. Instead of cutting the tag end at right angles, it should be cut on a 45° angle facing back toward the knot.

On knots that must pass through a guide repeatedly when casting or fighting a fish, veteran anglers have found that it pays to coat this knot with a rubber-based cement such as Pliobond. The cement can be tapered over the knot and, when it hardens, it will protect the strands from nicking or catching on a guide.

Knot Parts

To facilitate understanding the step-by-step tying instructions for each knot, it is important that you become familiar with the following terms and their definitions:

TAG END—The part of the line in which the knot is tied. Think of it as the *short* end of the line. Tag end will also be used to denote the short excess line that remains after a knot is tied. This would normally be the portion that is trimmed.

STANDING PART—The main part of the line as distinguished from the tag end. This would be the line that goes to the reel or the longer end if you are working with leader material.

TURNS OR WRAPS—For our purposes, consider a turn or wrap to be one complete revolution of line around another. It is normally achieved by passing the tag end around the standing part or a standing loop.

LOOP—Technically, a loop is a closed curve of line. It can be formed by bringing the tag end back and alongside the standing part or by tying a knot that creates a loop.

DOUBLE LINE—A double line is similar to a loop except that both strands of line are used together instead of working with the loop that is formed. If you were to pinch the round end of a loop shut with your fingers, you would create a double line. A double line is also fashioned with certain knots such as the Bimini Twist.

THE OVERHAND KNOT—*Breaking strength 40%–75%*

By itself, the Overhand Knot is the weakest and poorest knot you can use. It is used, however, to form portions of more sophisticated knots and for that reason, we are illustrating it. Remember that a wind knot created by improper fly casting is an overhand knot and will considerably weaken the line. Since the Overhand Knot is well known and simple to tie, it's a good place to begin. The instructions will help you to become familiar with the pattern of steps we will outline for each knot.

1. Hold the standing part of the line between the thumb and forefinger of the left hand about eight inches from the end. The tag end is held between the thumb and forefinger of your right hand. Bring your right hand toward your left hand so that the tag end lies against the standing part of the line forming a loop.

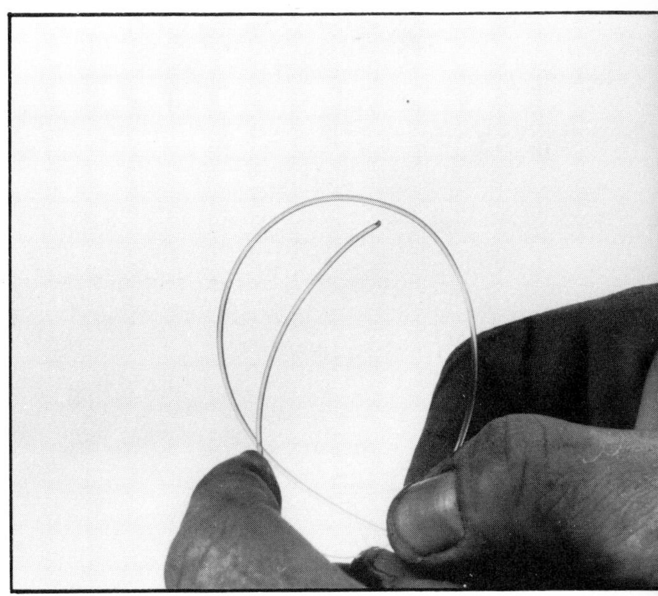

2. Slide the loop formed in Step 1 under the thumb and forefinger of your left hand and hold it firmly. With your right hand, pass the tag end over the standing part and then slip it through the loop.

3. Note that the tag end passes over the standing part and through the loop. Grasp the tag end in your right hand and the standing part in your left hand. Moisten the knot and use a steady pull to tighten.

THE BIMINI TWIST—*Breaking strength 100% (Also called Twenty Times Around Knot, Double Line Loop)*

This is the most important knot you can learn, because it is the basis of most knot-tying systems. The Bimini Twist can be tied in monofilament or braided line with 100% knot strength, forming a double line with a loop that becomes stronger than the standing part of the single line.

Unless you are in a fishing situation that dictates no leader and a delicate presentation, the Bimini Twist should automatically be tied in the tag end of any braided or monofilament line. As soon as you load a reel spool with line, put a Bimini Twist in the end and you're ready to create a knot system.

The uses of the Bimini are limitless. It is the primary knot for making a double line on offshore trolling reels. It can also be used to fashion a shock leader for casting, for making your own fly leaders, or for any assignment in which you want 100% efficiency from your knots.

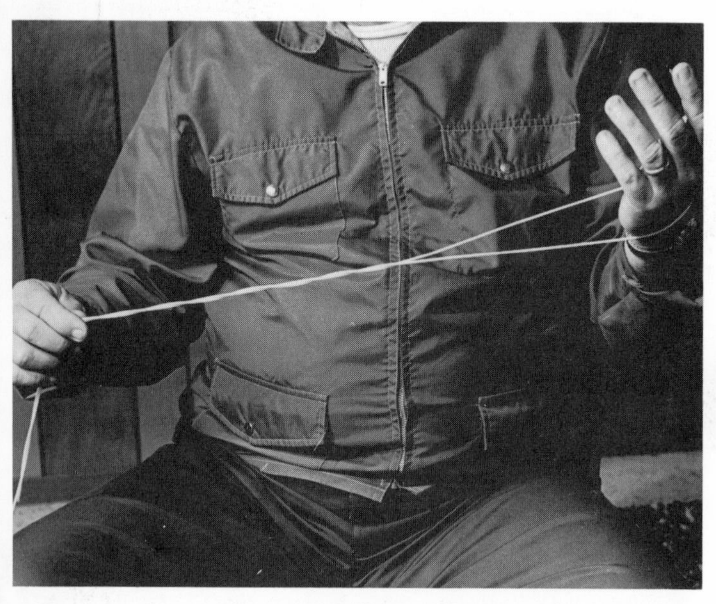

1. Measure six feet of line and double the tag end of the line back against the standing part. Grasp the standing part and the tag end securely between the thumb and forefinger of your left hand so that the loop formed is two feet long. Slip your right hand through the loop. Twist your right hand twenty times, placing twenty twists in the loop. The left hand must hold both strands of the line firmly, preventing the twists from sliding past that point.

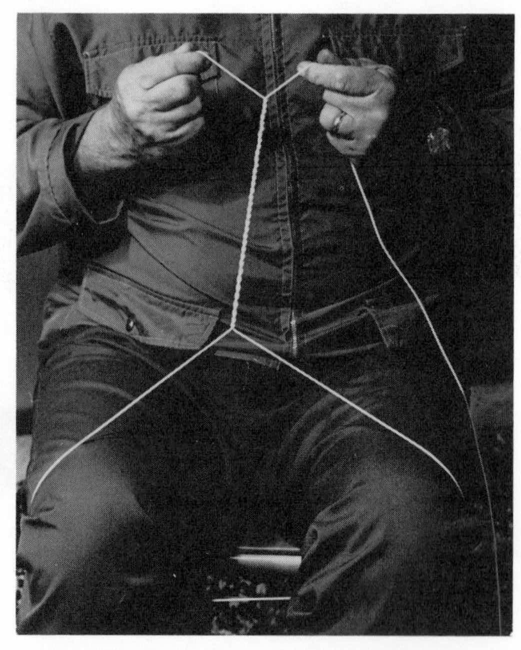

2. Holding the line as indicated in Step 1 (remember the line has twenty twists), slide it over your legs and around your knees as illustrated. Make sure *all* the twists remain in the line. Now take the tag end in your right hand and the standing part in your left hand. Pull both evenly, forcing the twists together as shown. Look at the photo closely. Note that the tag end and the standing part are each at about a 45° angle to the twists (90° total angle). This is important. Most beginners have the tendency of pulling the tag end and standing part down, forming a much greater angle (up to 90° *on each side*). This, in turn, causes the twists to jump and you won't get them to tighten evenly.

3. When the twists have been forced tight, you may have to adjust your grip on the two lines, but the tag end remains in your right hand and the standing part in your left hand. This is important! Move the standing part of the line (your left hand) toward a vertical position, but keep the line slightly canted to maintain tension. At the same time, move the tag end of the line at about a 90° angle to the twists (your right hand). The tag end of the line must roll over the first twist, jumping the point where the twists begin.

4. If you've done it correctly up to this point, this is what the knot should look like when the first roll of the tag end has crossed over the twists.

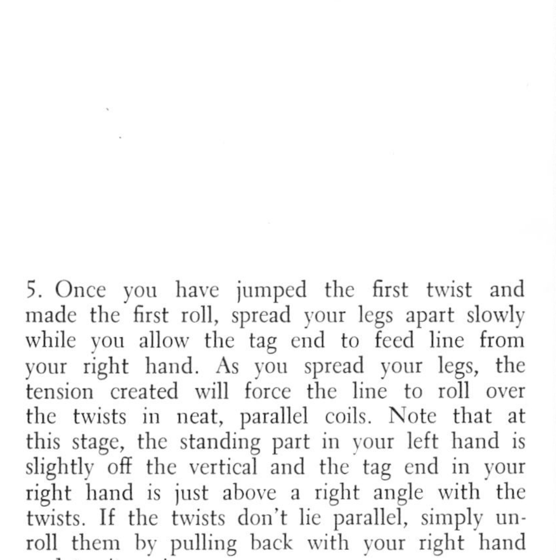

5. Once you have jumped the first twist and made the first roll, spread your legs apart slowly while you allow the tag end to feed line from your right hand. As you spread your legs, the tension created will force the line to roll over the twists in neat, parallel coils. Note that at this stage, the standing part in your left hand is slightly off the vertical and the tag end in your right hand is just above a right angle with the twists. If the twists don't lie parallel, simply unroll them by pulling back with your right hand and try it again.

6. At the end of the roll-over procedure, the knot should look like this.

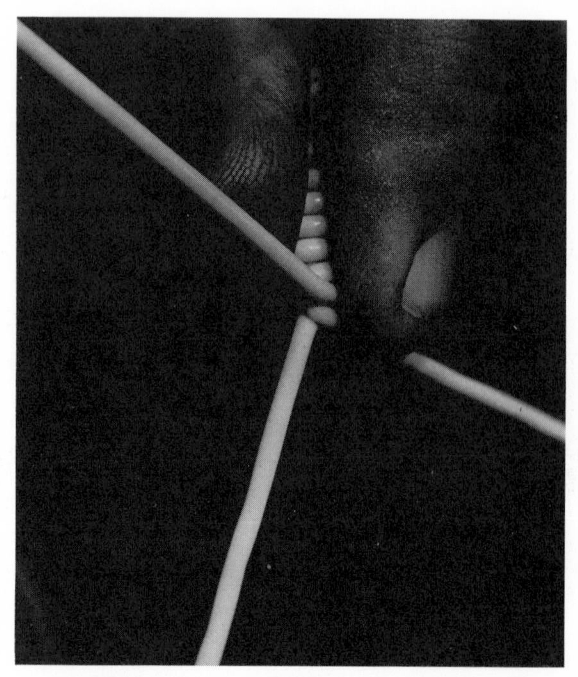

7. Without moving your legs and while maintaining tension on both the tag end and the standing part of the line, work your left hand down and grasp the knot between the thumb and forefinger as shown. You must maintain tension or the knot will fall apart. It takes a little practice to achieve the digital dexterity necessary to maintain tension while moving your hand, so don't become discouraged.

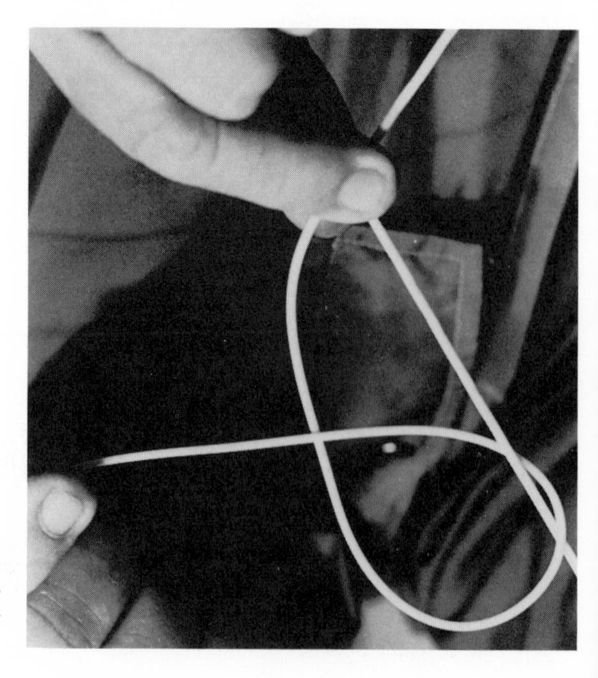

8. Pinching the knot with your left hand (Step 7), make an overhand knot with the tag end around the nearer side of the loop (actually a half hitch).

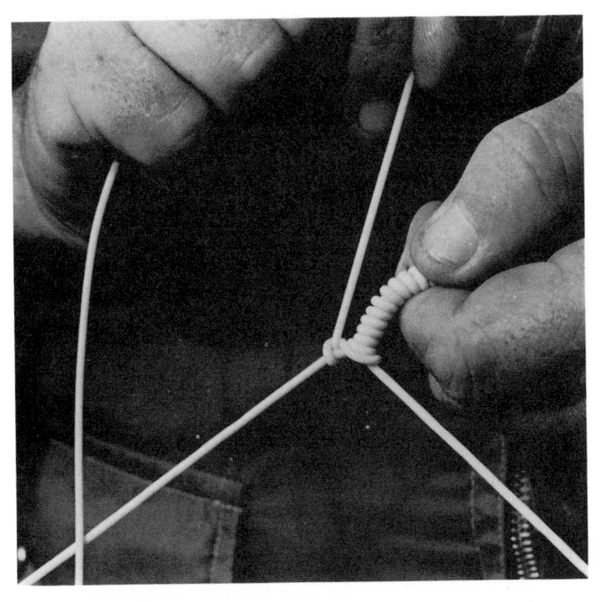

9. Pull the tag end toward you with the right hand, tightening the half hitch against the roll-over portion of the knot. At this point, you can release all pressure and remove the line from under your knees. The knot will not come undone.

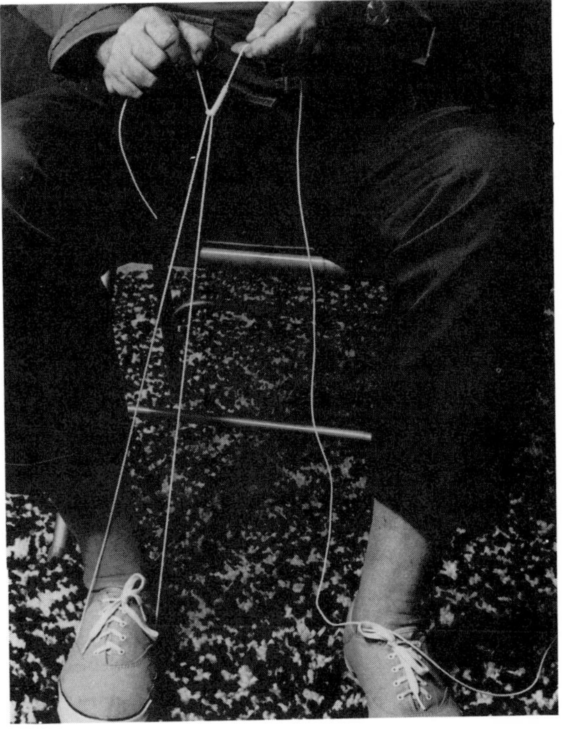

10. Slip your right foot in the loop. Hold the tag end in your right hand and the standing part in your left hand.

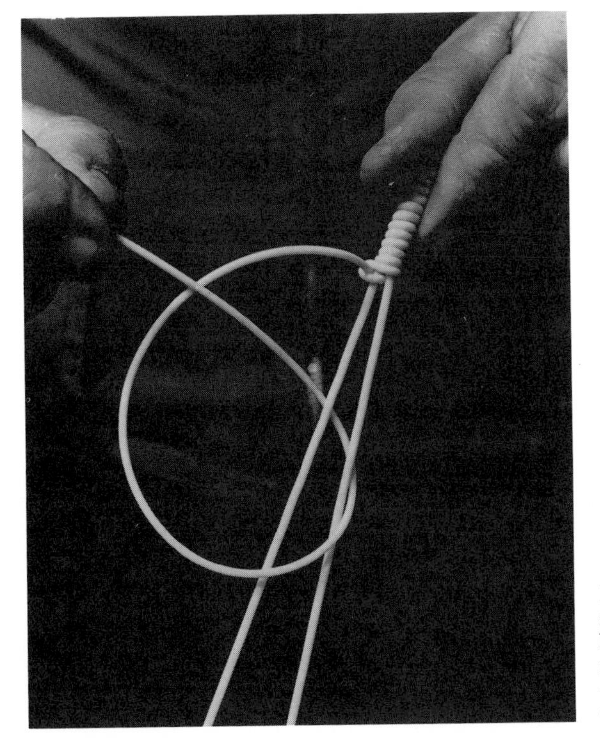

11. Take the tag end and put it around *both* standing parts of the loop, pulling it through the loop just created to form another half hitch. *Do not draw it tight!* Instead, make two more turns with the tag end around *both* standing parts of the loop.

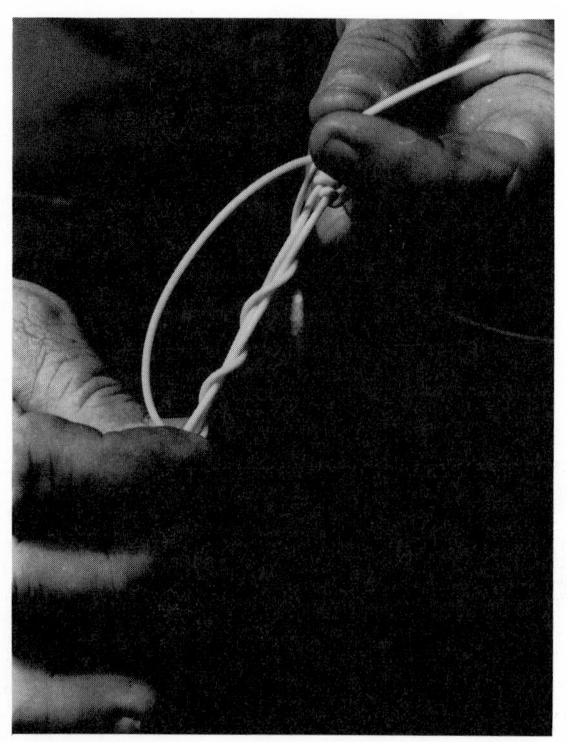

12. This is the way the knot will look after you have made the three turns outlined in Step 11.

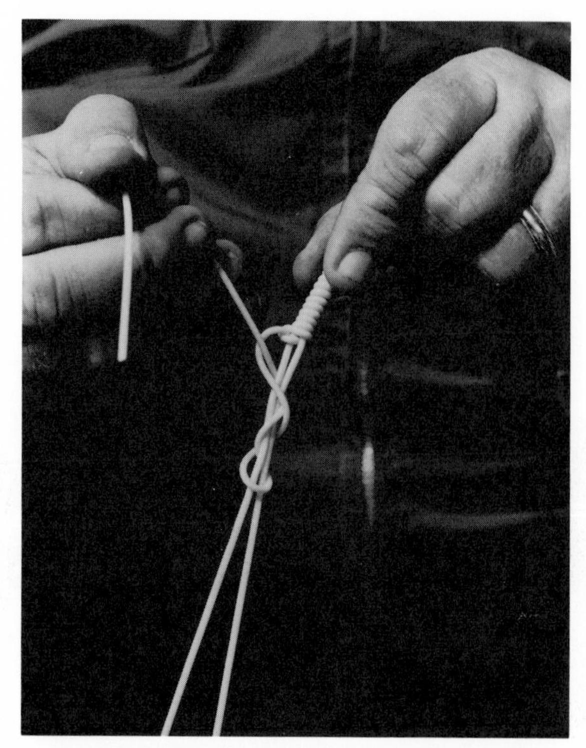

13. Tighten the knot by drawing carefully on the tag end. You'll find that you will probably have to keep pushing the three turns you made in Step 11 away from the knot as you continue to pull on the tag end. Eventually, you can work them up evenly against the roll-over section of the knot to lock it permanently.

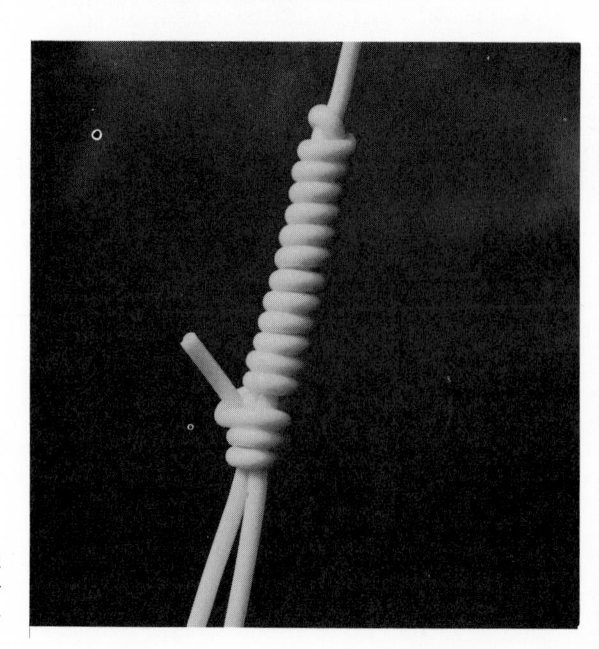

14. The Bimini Twist should *always* be trimmed with about ¼ inch of the tag end extending outside the knot. The finished knot looks like this.

We have tried to lead you through the easiest method of *learning* the Bimini Twist, so that you can develop a feel for the more difficult aspects. After you can handle this knot without difficulty in the manner we have outlined, you might want to progress to a quicker way of tying it. We must also remind you that if you want to make a long double line, you will need someone else to hold the line for you just behind the point you want the knot to be. Your helper will also make the twists while you hold the tag end against the standing part. That's how fifteen- and thirty-foot sections of double line are made for trolling purposes. Now to that quicker way of tying the Bimini:

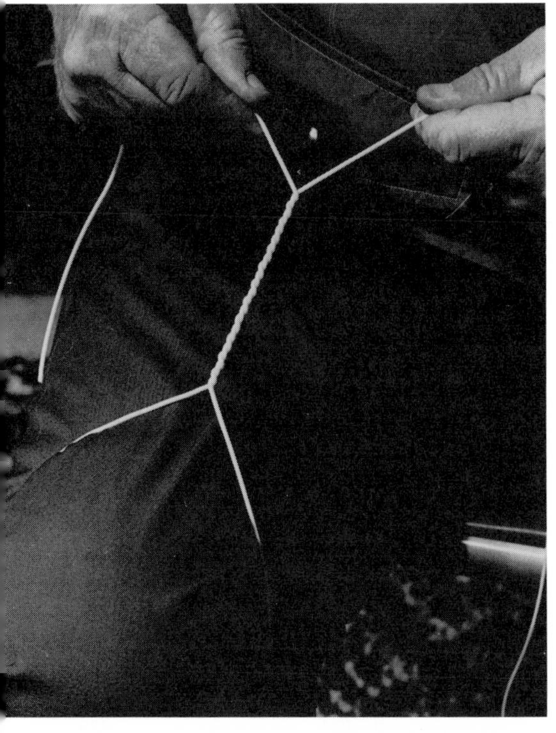

15. The slowest part of tying the knot as illustrated above is slipping your legs through the loop. Instead, place the loop over your bent knee and draw the twists tight the same as you did before.

16. In the first method, you applied tension by spreading your knees apart (*See* Photo 3), so that your right hand remained free to feed the tag end of the line as it flowed around the tightened twists. If you place the loop over your knee, you must learn to feed line with your thumb and third finger of the right hand, while your forefinger pushes upward at the junction of the standing legs of the loop. Your forefinger now does what your legs did in the original tying method.

Tying to a Hook or Connector

IMPROVED CLINCH KNOT—*Breaking strength 95%*

The Improved Clinch Knot is one of the all-time favorites for tying line to a hook, lure, or swivel. There are many who rate it at almost 100% breaking strength, but we prefer to view this knot slightly on the conservative side and call it a 95% knot.

The most critical aspect of the Improved Clinch Knot is how many turns you take around the standing part. Extensive research by several independent sources has demonstrated that five turns are the correct number. If you use less than five turns, you sacrifice knot strength; and if you exceed five, it becomes increasingly difficult to tighten the knot properly. When a knot isn't completely tightened, it will slip under pressure and then break.

If you are using a single strand of relatively light monofilament, it pays to double that light strand before tying the knot. With very heavy leader material, the 3½ Turn Clinch Knot is the answer.

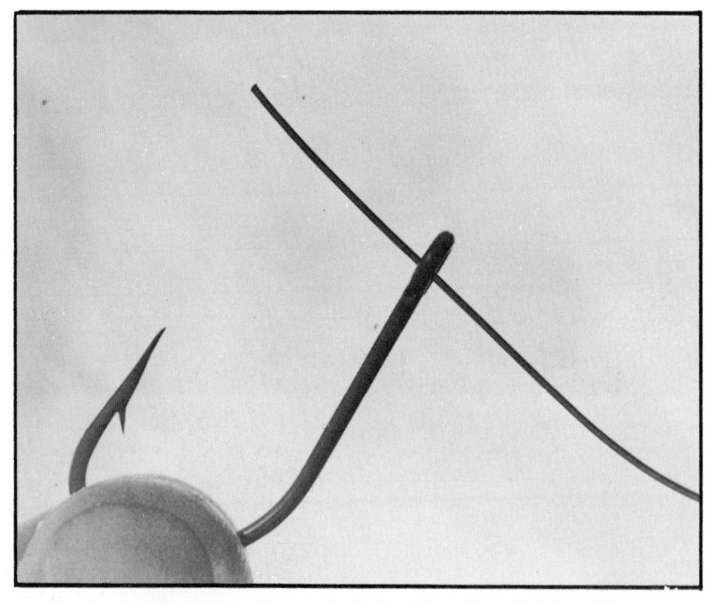

1. Insert the tag end of the line through the eye of the hook, leaving about six or eight inches to tie the knot.

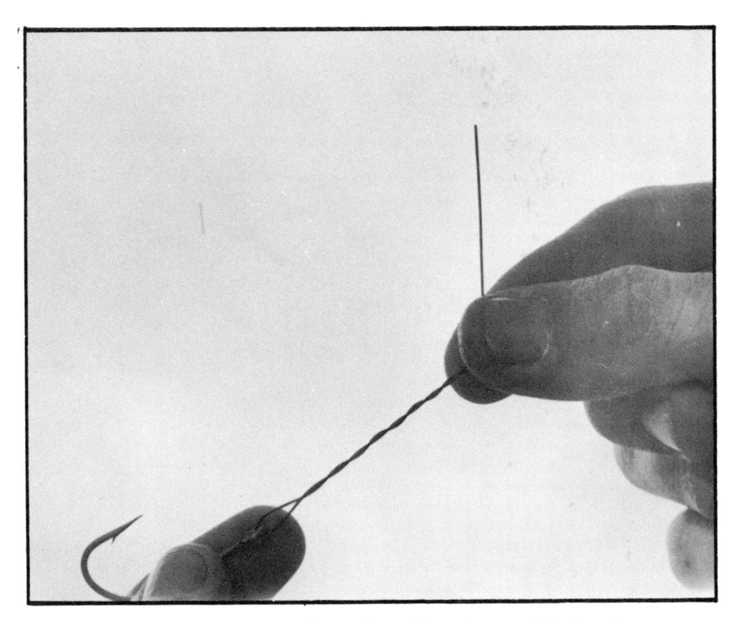

2. Hold the hook in the palm of your left hand, gripping it with the last three fingers of that hand. Hold the standing part of the line across the palm of your right hand and grip it with the last three fingers of your right hand. Use the thumb and first finger of each hand to make *five turns* with the tag end around the standing part.

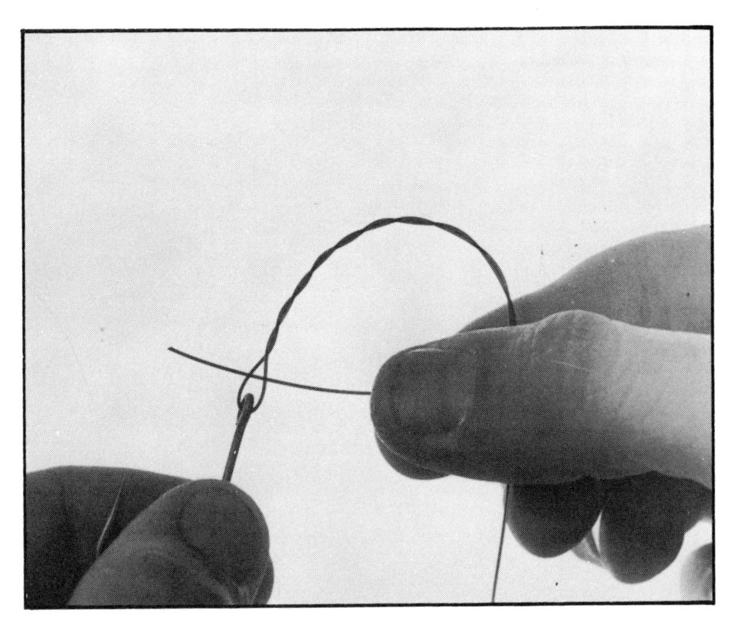

3. Change the grip on the hook with your left hand to expose the loop formed between the eye of the hook and the first turn around the standing part of the line. With your right hand, insert the tag end of the line through this loop and grip the tag end with the thumb and forefinger of your left hand.

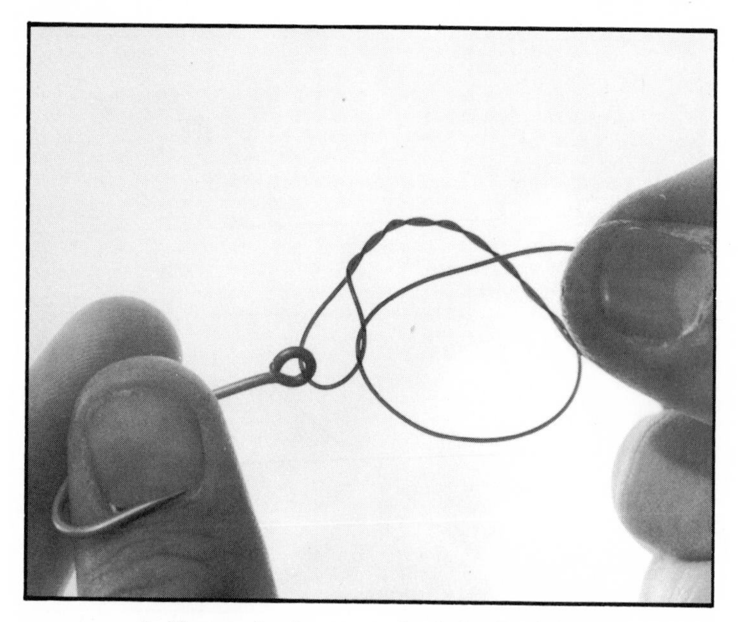

4. Now push the tag end of the line through the loop that was just formed by the tag end and the twisted standing part. This will increase the strength of the knot by 30% over a regular Clinch Knot.

5. Moisten the knot and pull steadily to tighten. Trim the tag end and the finished knot will look like this.

3½ TURN CLINCH KNOT

The 3½ Turn Clinch Knot is tied exactly the same way as the regular Clinch Knot except for the number of turns around the standing part of the line. It is used only when a heavy monofilament shock leader is employed (exceeding sixty-pound test), because a five-turn Clinch Knot cannot be tightened properly.

1. Insert the tag end of the leader through the eye of the hook, leaving eight to ten inches to tie the knot.

2. Bring the tag end of the line between the forefinger of your right hand and the standing part of the line.

3. Take 3½ full turns around the standing part of the line.

4. Push the tag end of the leader through the loop created at the eye of the hook just before the first turn.

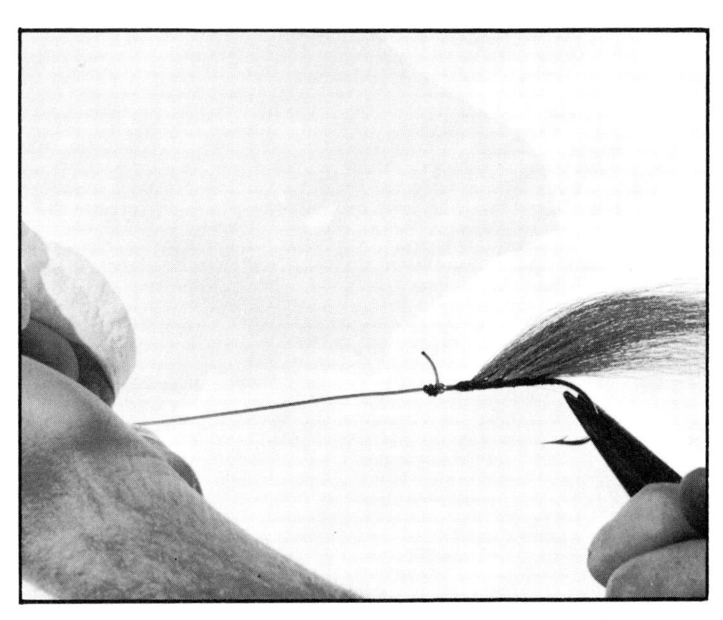

5. With heavy monofilament, you cannot pull this knot tight with your bare hands. Use a handkerchief or rag around your left hand to grip the standing part of the line. Hold the hook with pliers. Lubricate the knot and pull steadily until the knot is tightened.

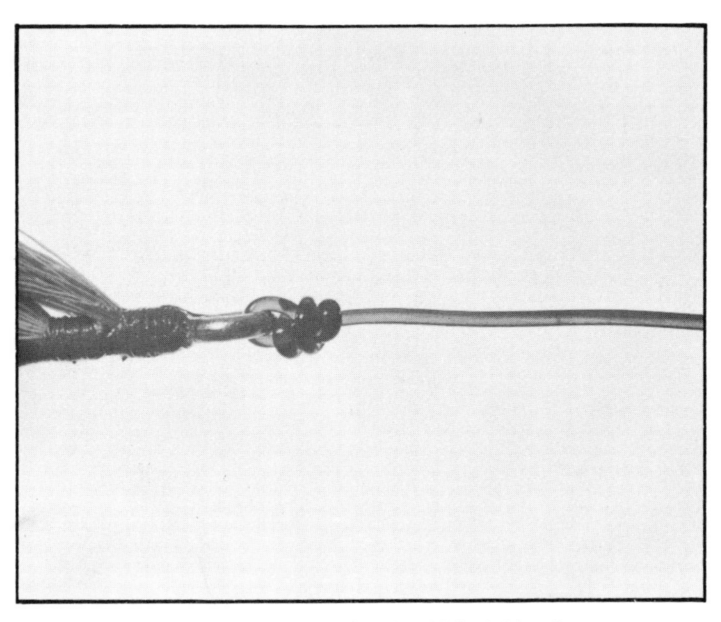

6. Trim the knot and it should look like this.

PALOMAR KNOT—*Breaking strength 95%–100%*

For many people, the Palomar Knot is easier to tie than the Improved Clinch Knot, and if you tie the Palomar properly, you can achieve 100% knot strength. Like the Clinch Knot, it is used to attach a hook, swivel, lure, or sinker to the line.

1. Double the tag end back against the standing part and insert the double line through the eye of the hook.

2. Tie a simple overhand knot with the double line, but don't tighten it.

3. Slip the loop over the hook while holding the overhand knot in place.

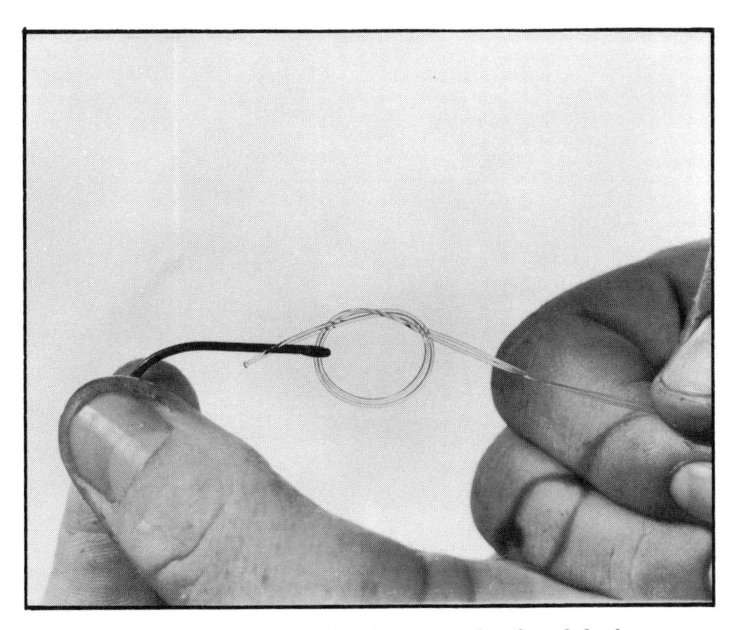

4. Hold the hook firmly in one hand and both the tag end and standing part of the line in the other. Pull steadily to tighten the knot, being careful that the loop slips past the eye of the hook before final tightening.

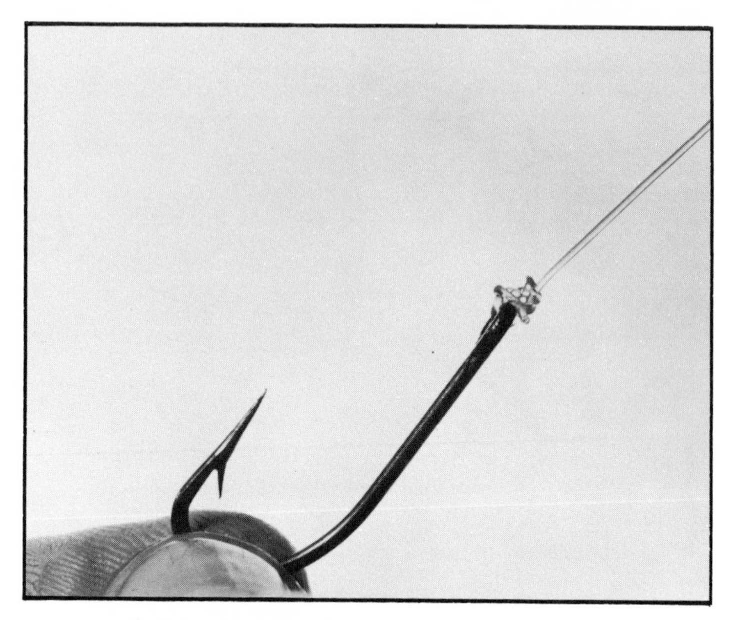

5. Trim the tag end and the knot is completed.

JANSIK SPECIAL—*Breaking strength 98%–100%*

Although the Jansik Special is not well known, it is one of the best ways to tie a single strand of light monofilament to a hook, swivel, or lure. You can use it effectively with monofilament lines testing up to twenty pounds.

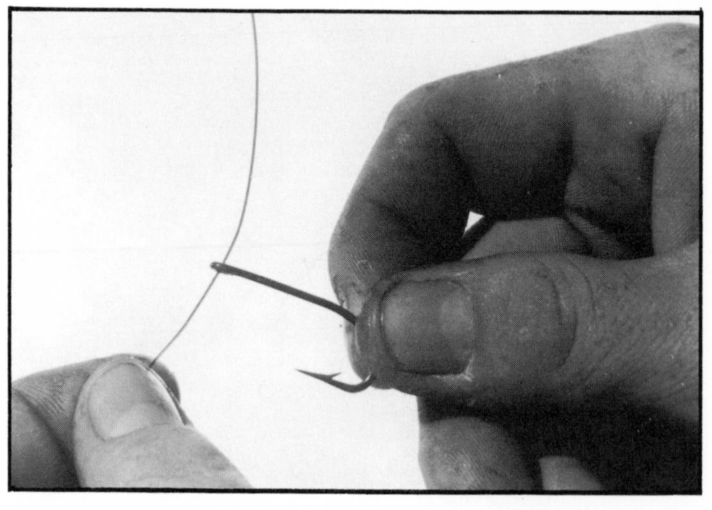

1. Insert the tag end of the monofilament through the eye of the hook or lure. The tag end should be about a foot long.

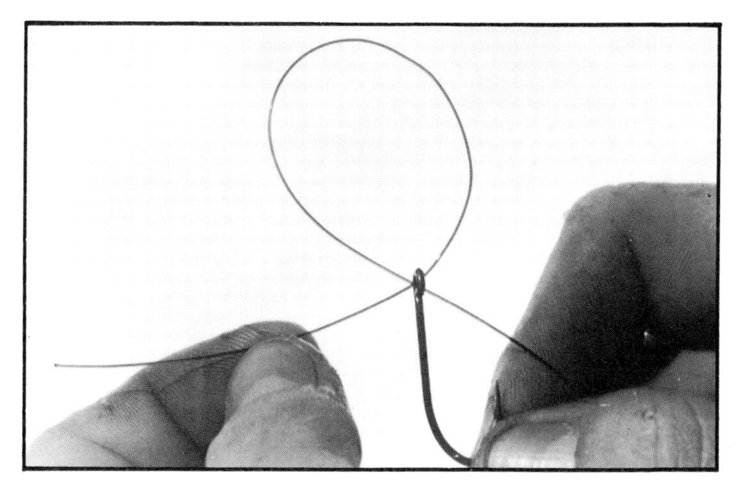

2. Bring the tag end around and through the eye of the hook forming a loop.

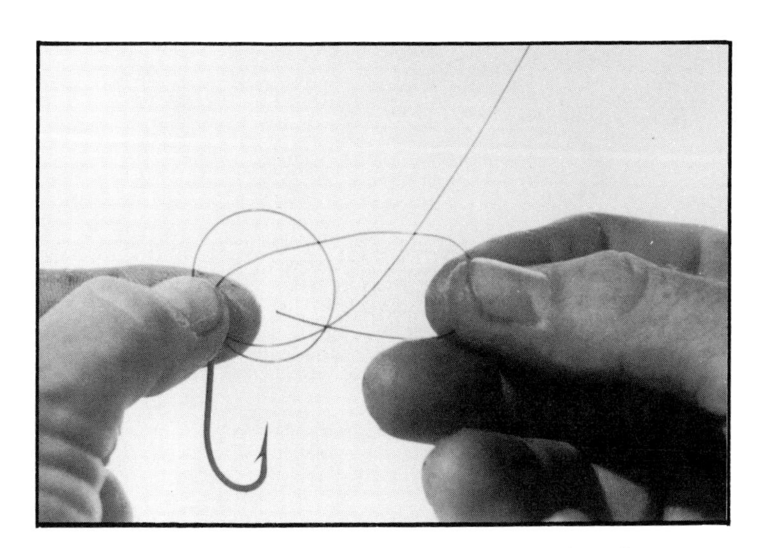

3. Hold the loop in place with the thumb and forefinger of your left hand and insert the tag end of the line through the eye of the hook once more. As you look at the knot in this stage, you have two complete parallel loops with the standing part of the line going into the eye of the hook and the tag end coming out of the eye. Lay the standing part of the line against the two loops so that you are holding three pieces of monofilament together between the thumb and forefinger of your left hand. Now bring the tag end around to close the third loop as if you were going to insert it into the eye of the hook again. Instead, wrap the tag end around the three pieces of monofilament three times.

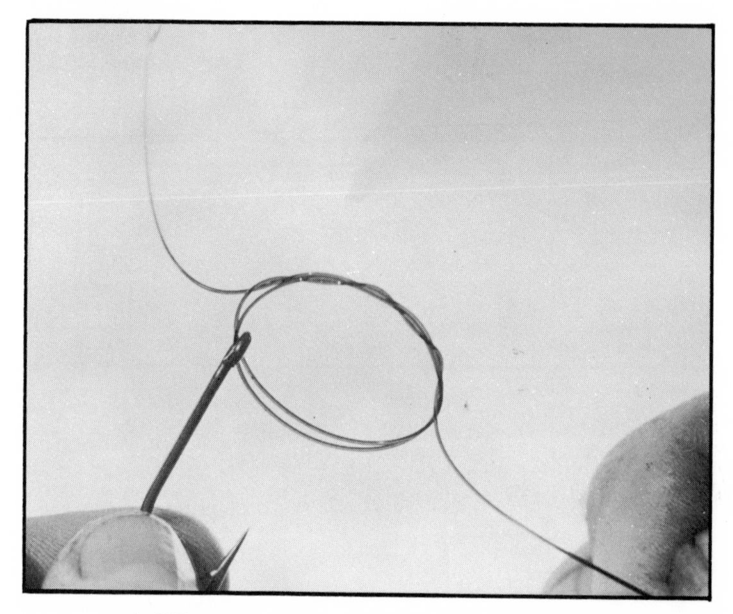

4. When you have completed Step 3, the knot should look like this. To tighten, moisten the knot with saliva or water. Grip the hook with pliers and hold the standing part of the line in your hand. Put the tag end of the line in your teeth. Now pull all three points (hook, standing part, and tag end) together with steady pressure. The knot will tighten neatly. Trim it and you're ready to fish.

CRAWFORD KNOT—*Breaking strength 95%*

Here's another way of tying monofilament to a hook, swivel, or lure. It has excellent knot strength and is relatively easy to tie.

1. Hold the hook in your left hand and insert the tag end of the line or leader through the eye of the hook. Allow at least eight inches of line to tie the knot. Then pass the tag end behind the standing part to form a loop.

2. Working from the standing part toward the eye of the hook, pass the tag end around both legs of the loop that was formed in Step 1.

3. The line forming the knot should be held in your left hand. Use your right hand to bring the tag end across the front of the loop. You are forming a figure eight.

4. Now tuck the tag end between the top of the loop and the standing part of the line. Hold the loop just above the hook eye and pull on the tag end. This will tighten the knot. When the knot has been tightened, release your grip on the tag end and hold the standing part. Pull on the standing part and the knot will slide down to the hook eye. Trim the tag end.

IMPROVED TURLE KNOT—*Breaking strength* 75%–85%

The Improved Turle Knot lacks the strength of the Improved Clinch Knot and other methods for tying a line to a hook, but it was designed solely for a special situation. A number of flies are tied on hooks with turned-down eyes. If you were to use a regular knot, the pull on the hook would be offset instead of straight. Particularly with dry flies, this would have a tendency to stand the fly on its nose. The Turle Knot creates a straight pull on any hook with a turned-down eye.

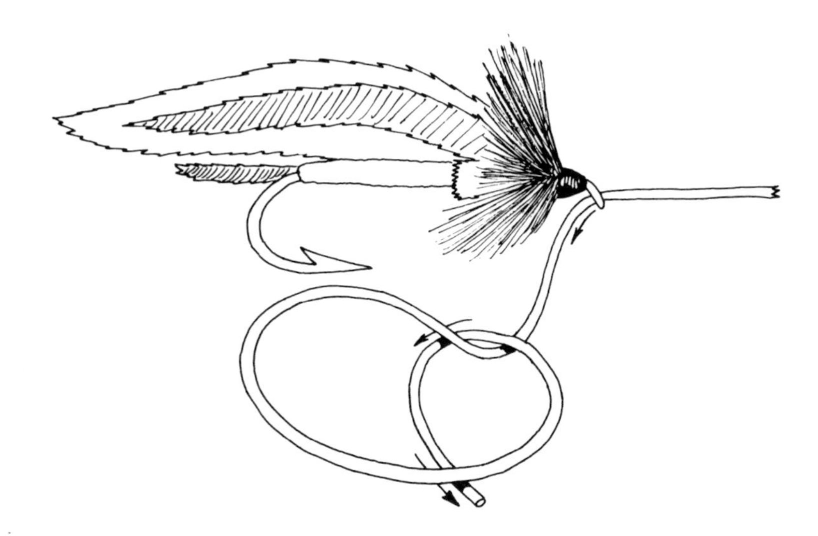

1. Insert the tag end of the leader through the eye of the hook so that it passes from the top of the eye toward the bottom. Allow yourself about a foot of leader to tie the knot. You'll gain most of this back when the knot is tightened. Then pass the tag end of the leader around the standing part to form a loop as illustrated.

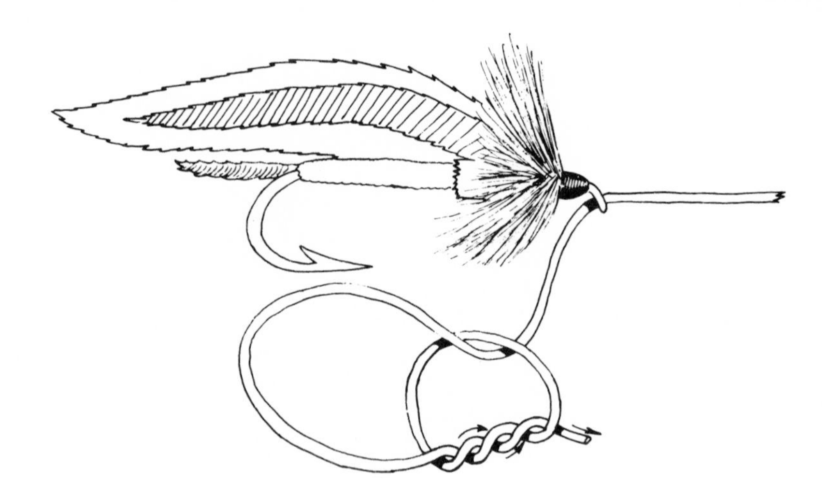

2. Insert the tag end through the smaller loop you created in Step 1. Then insert it a second time.

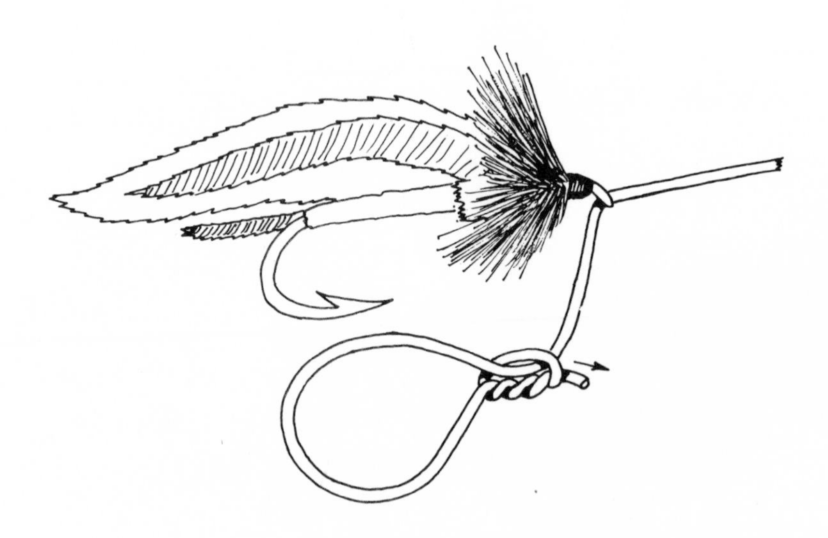

3. Hold the tag end in one hand and one leg of the big loop in the other. Pull both hands apart to tighten the Slip Knot you made.

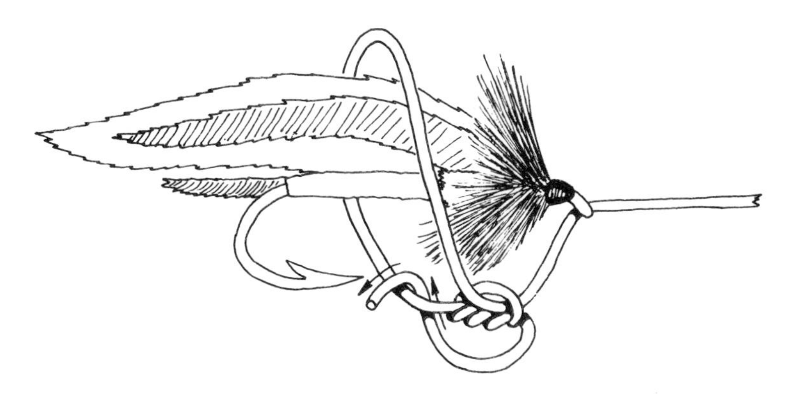

4. Pass the big loop over the fly, working from the tail of the fly toward the head. As the loop clears the fly, you can take one turn around a leg of the loop with the tag end of the leader. This gives you a little extra strength in the knot.

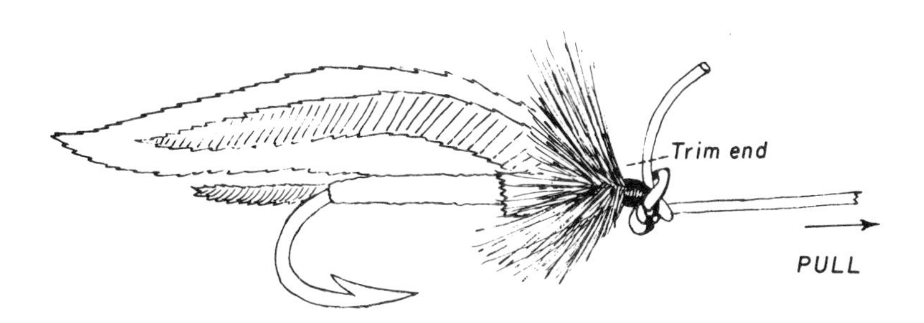

5. Tighten the knot carefully by pulling slowly on the standing part. The trick is to make certain the loop clears the hackles on the fly. When the knot is tightened, the slip knot portion will jam under the eye of the hook and the loop that passed over the fly will seat across the eye.

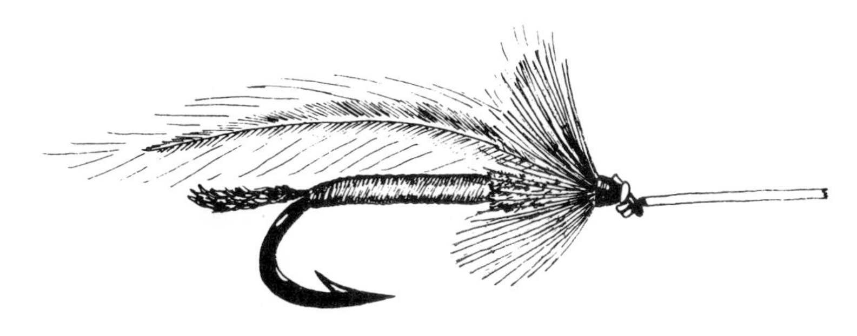

6. The finished knot will enable you to exert a straight and level pull on the fly.

SNELLING A HOOK

Snelling a hook provides a strong connection when the angler is fishing with bait and when he is using a separate length of leader. You cannot snell a hook with line attached on one end to a reel.

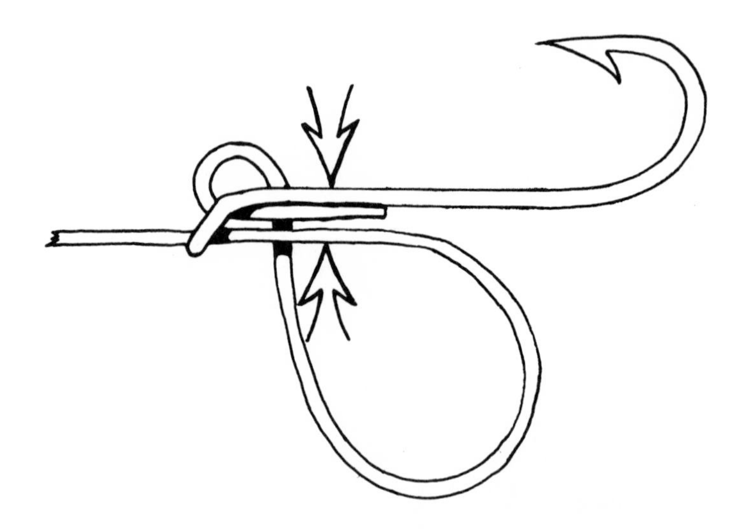

1. Insert one end of the leader through the eye of the hook so that it extends from one to two inches past the eye. Insert the other end of the leader through the eye of the hook in the opposite direction. This second end will point toward the bend and barb of the hook. Hold the hook and the leader ends securely between the thumb and forefinger of your left hand. The entire length of the leader will belly below the hook in a large loop. Now take the leg of this loop that is closer to the eye of the hook in your right hand. Wrap it over the hook shank and both ends of the leader, making each turn *away* from you. You will be wrapping consecutive turns *from the hook eye toward the hook bend.*

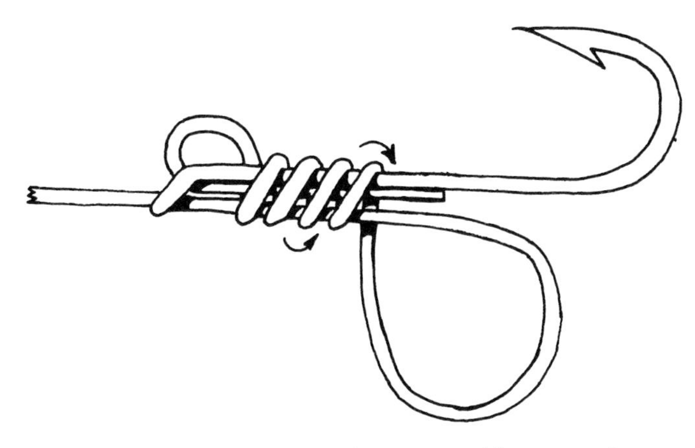

2. Continue wrapping for seven or eight turns and then hold the wraps in place with the thumb and forefinger of your left hand.

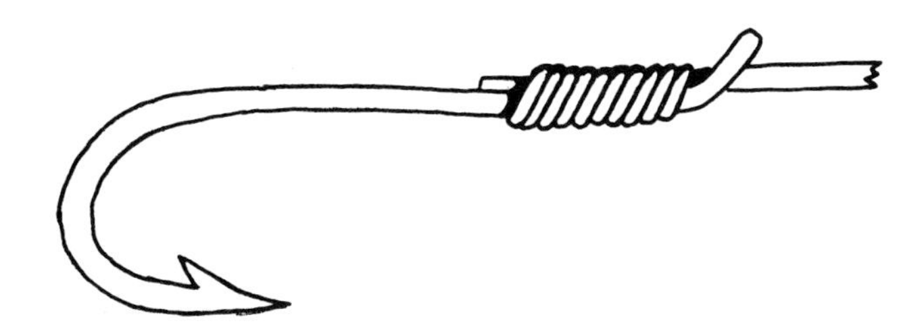

3. As you hold the turns in place with your left hand, grip the end of the leader that is protruding through the eye of the hook in your right hand and pull slowly and steadily. You must hold the turns with your left hand or the knot will unravel. Continue pulling on this end until the entire loop passes under and through the turns. When the knot is semi-tight, use your fingers to slide it up against the eye of the hook. Then, grip the short end lying along the shank of the hook with a pair of pliers. Pull on this end and the standing part together to completely tighten the knot. Trim the short end and the hook is snelled. Some people snell a hook by simply laying the second end along the shank of the hook and not passing it through the eye (only one end through the eye). Both methods work equally well.

OFFSHORE SWIVEL KNOT—*Breaking strength 95%–100%*

Designed originally to attach a swivel securely to the double line used in offshore big-game trolling, the Swivel Knot can also be used for attaching a hook. It has excellent applications when fishing natural bait in shallow water for such species as bonefish and permit. The main feature of this knot is that if one strand breaks, the other strand will not slip. Before tying the Swivel Knot, a Bimini Twist should be placed in the line first.

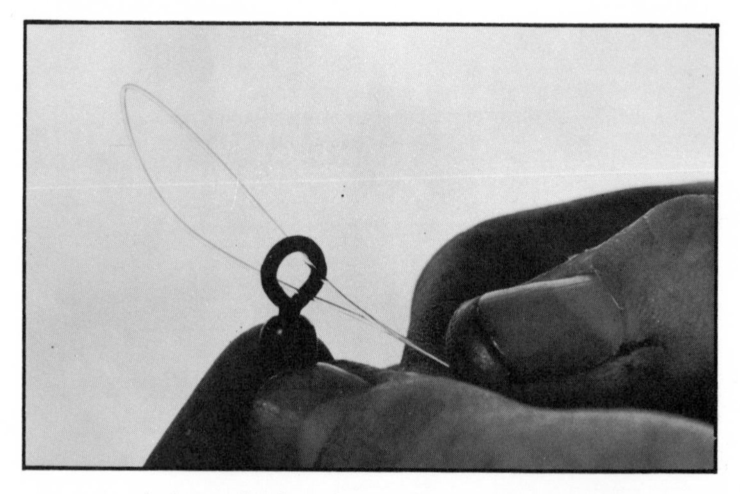

1. Insert the loop from a Bimini Twist through the eye of the swivel (or hook).

2. After the loop has been passed through the eye of the swivel, place the fingers of the left hand inside the loop while holding both strands with your right hand. The swivel hangs loosely between your two hands.

3. Rotate your left hand one half turn so that you place a twist in the loop end between the left hand and the swivel.

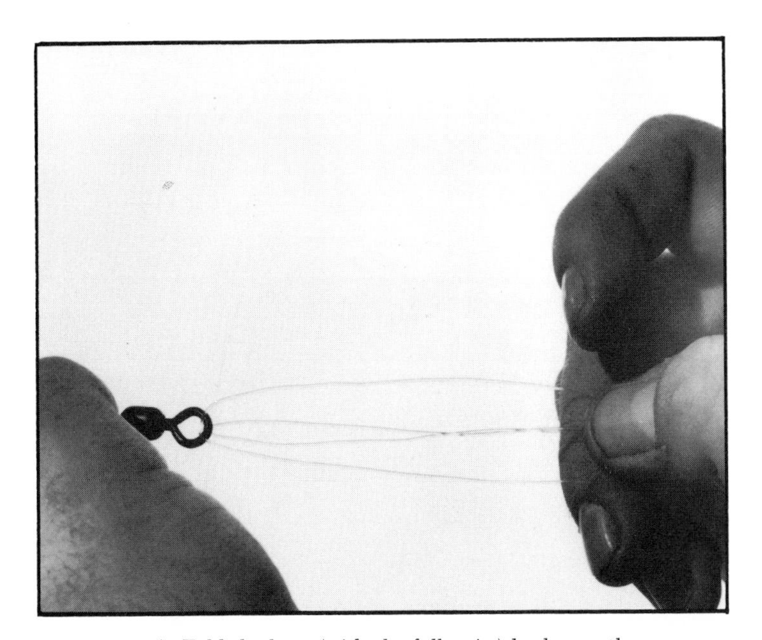

4. Fold the loop (with the full twist) back over the swivel and place the end of that loop in your right hand. The right hand now holds the end of the loop plus both strands of that loop which actually forms the equivalent of a second loop. Take the swivel in your left hand.

5. With the left hand, the swivel is pushed through the center of both loops (toward the right hand). This procedure is repeated until the swivel has passed through the loops at least six times.

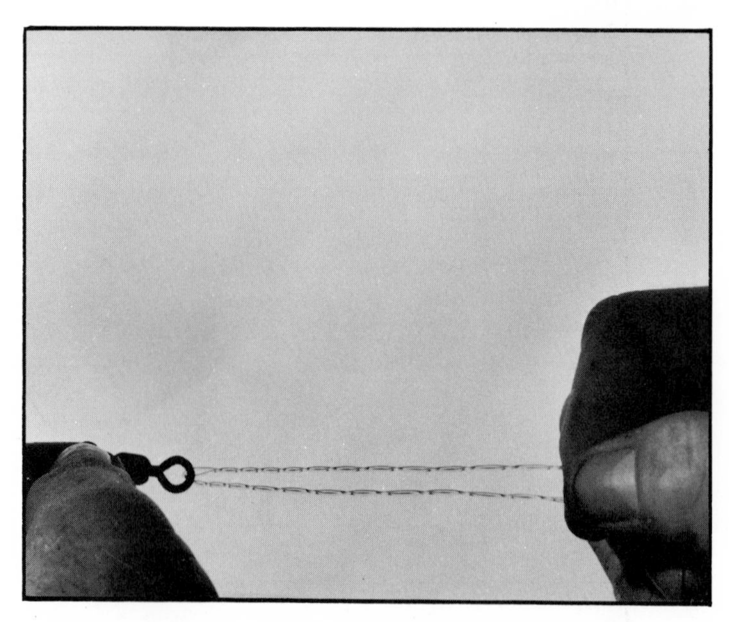

6. This is what the knot looks like when the swivel has been passed through the loops six times.

7. Hold the swivel firmly in your left hand and pull steadily on both strands of the standing part with your right hand. As you pull, the twists will start to work down toward the eye of the swivel.

8. It is almost impossible to draw this knot tight by simply pulling on the standing part. You'll probably have to grip the swivel with pliers and force the wraps toward the eye of the swivel with the thumb and forefinger.

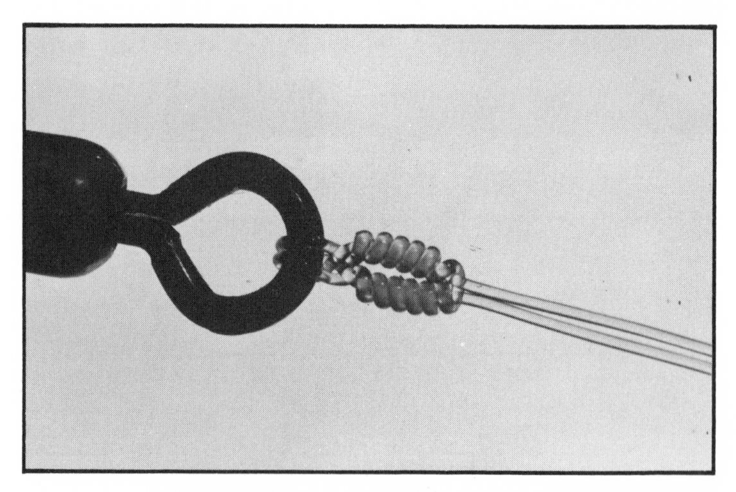

9. There is nothing to trim on the completed knot.

HOMER RHODE LOOP KNOT—*Breaking strength 50%–70%*

A favorite with many anglers because it can be tied quickly, the Homer Rhode Loop Knot can be used in monofilament and braided wire that is plastic coated. Because the breaking strength of this knot is low, it should only be tied when the breaking strength of the leader is at least *twice* that of the line being used. Normally, it is used to attach a lure to a heavy shock tippet being fished on light casting line. The advantage of this knot is that it enhances the action of the lure by creating a small loop that permits the lure to swing freely.

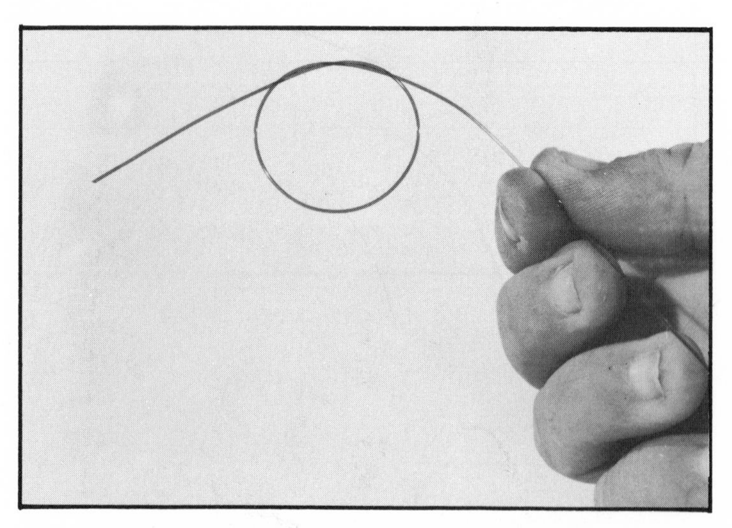

1. Put the lure down in front of you and tie an overhand knot with the tag end of the leader material.

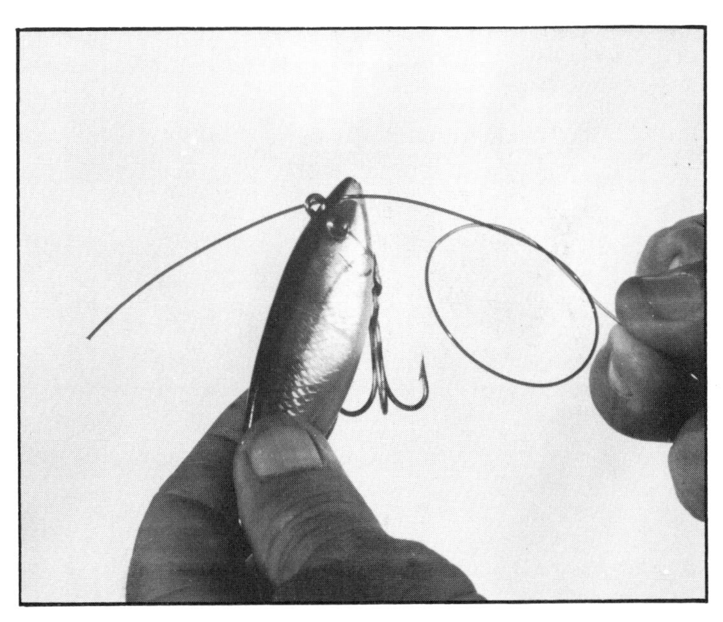

2. Insert the tag end of the leader through the eye of the lure.

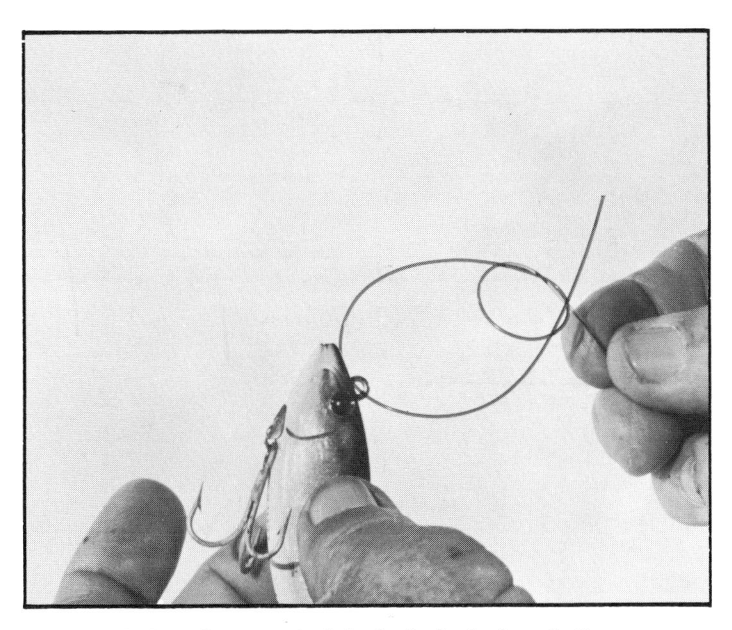

3. Pass the tag end of the leader back through the overhand knot.

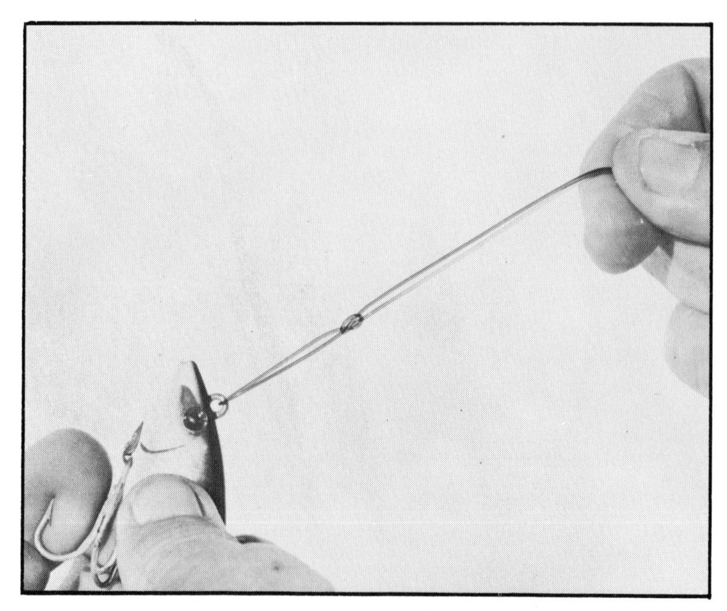

4. Hold the lure in your left hand and pull both the tag end and standing part together to close the overhand knot.

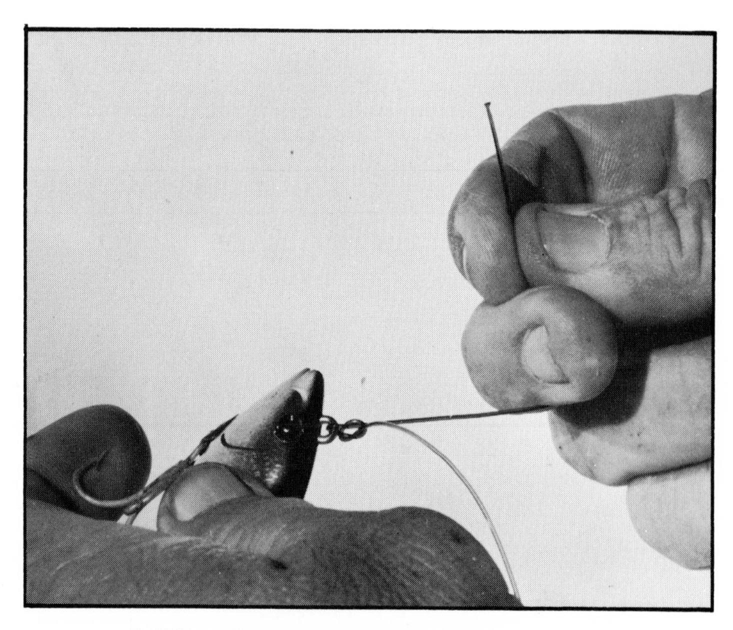

5. When the overhand knot has been closed, release the standing part and pull on the tag end. This will slide the overhand knot right down to the eye on the lure, enabling you to make a small, neat loop.

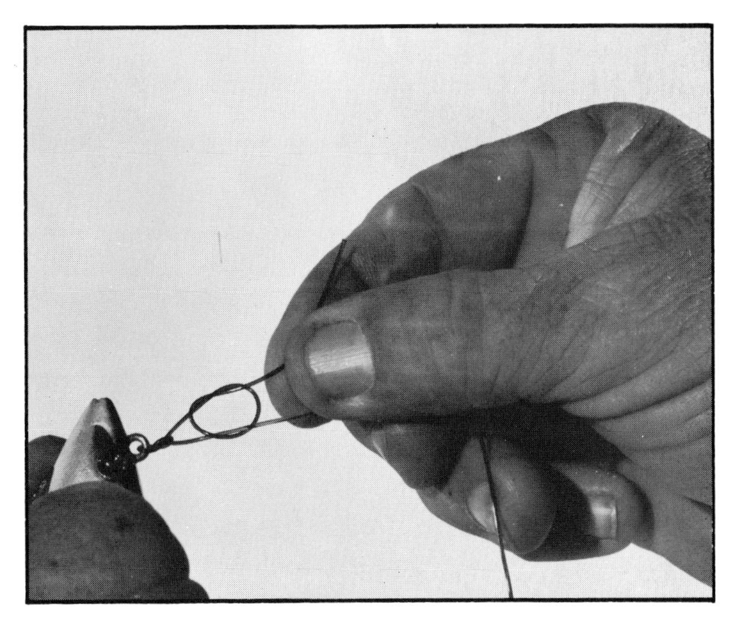

6. Using the tag end, tie a second overhand knot around the standing part as illustrated. The finished loop will form at about the spot where the second overhand knot is tied, so you can adjust loop size by calculating the spot where you will tighten the second overhand knot.

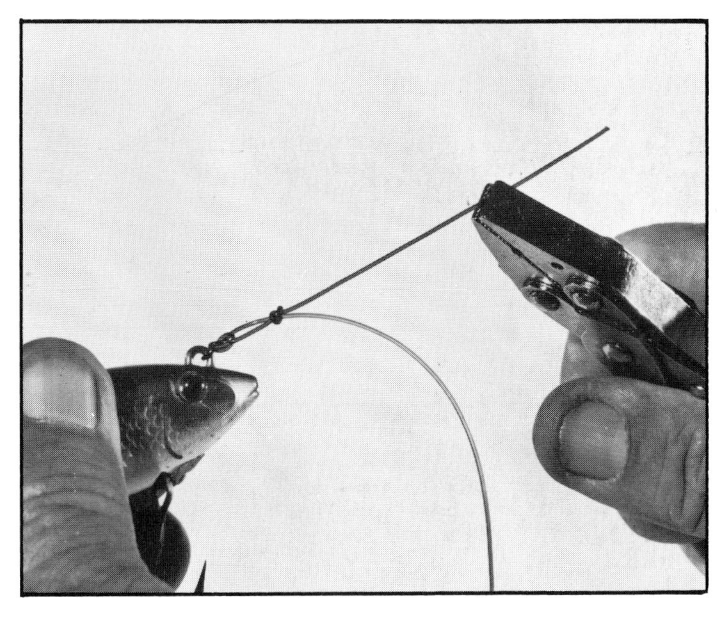

7. You will probably need pliers to close the second overhand knot tightly. Grasp the tag end with the pliers and pull. You may also have to hold the first overhand knot in place while you tighten the second.

8. When you have tightened the second overhand knot, hold the lure in one hand and pull the standing part of the line with the other. The first overhand knot will slide up the line and jam against the second overhand knot, completing your loop knot.

DUNCAN LOOP

The Duncan Loop is an excellent way to tie a leader to a hook or lure. It creates a sliding loop that permits the lure to have action in the water, but under pressure of a fish, the loop slides down and tightens. It's easy to tie and is a great knot for the artificial-lure angler.

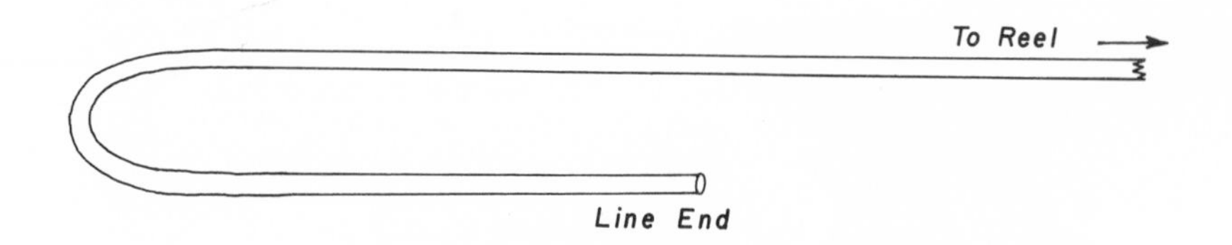

1. Pass the tag end of the monofilament through the eye of the hook or lure. Allow about eight inches of monofilament to tie the knot.

2. Bend the tag end of the monofilament back toward the hook eye to form a second loop. Then, take five turns around both legs of the first loop with the tag end. The tag end will pass inside of the second loop you created when you bent the mono back toward the hook eye.

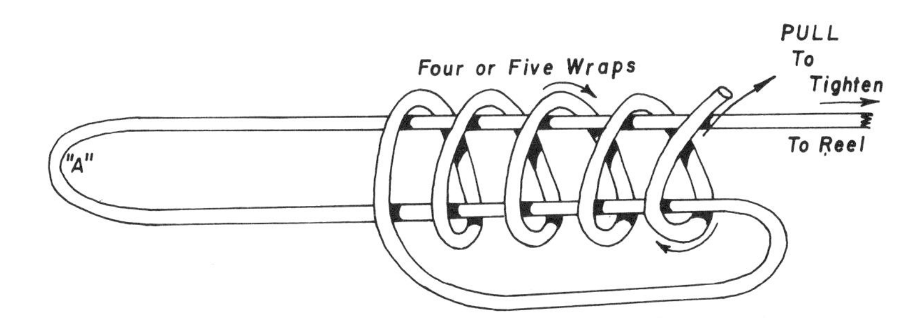

3. To tighten the knot, hold the hook or the loop at Point A. Pull on the tag end of the monofilament until the loop and the knot start to tighten. Then, slide the loop to the position you want and use pliers to pull on the tag end. This will tighten the knot securely. Under normal pressure, it will not slide, but if you are fighting a fish, the loop will slide down and tighten against the eye of the hook. When you have landed the fish, you can use your fingers to reopen the loop. Trim the tag end of the monofilament and the knot is completed.

TYING LINE TO REEL SPOOL

There are a number of methods for tying the end of monofilament or braided line around the hub of a reel spool. Our philosophy has always been that if a fish has taken all the line, a knot isn't going to hold him, so knot strength at this point is not critical. On the other hand, you do want something strong enough to hold in the event you lose a rod and reel overboard and have to pull it up by the line. If you're looking for a quick method to connect lines to reel spools, try this one.

1. Although the illustrations use a fly reel, the same method can be used on spinning or conventional reels. Pass the tag end of the line around the hub of the spool and bring it out again, making sure that the tag end and standing part are between the same set of reel pillars. Tie an overhand knot in the tag end of the line (*arrow*) and tighten it.

2. Using the tag end of the line, tie an overhand knot around the standing part as illustrated.

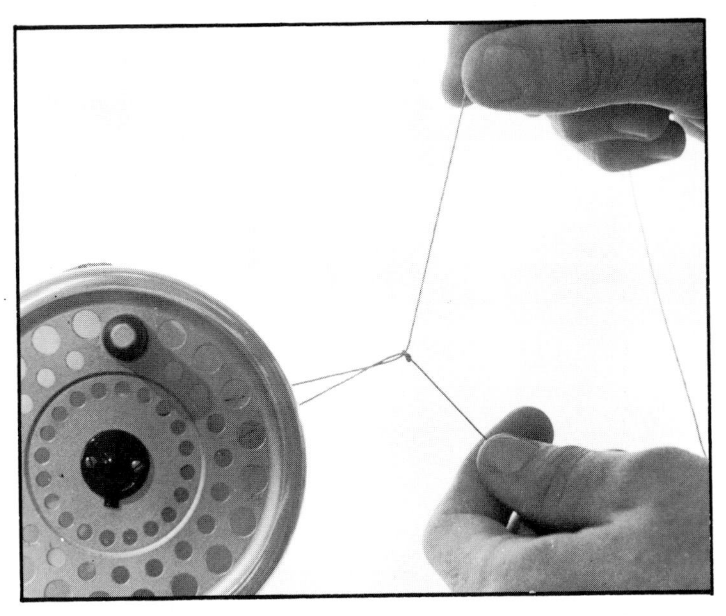

3. Draw the second overhand knot tight.

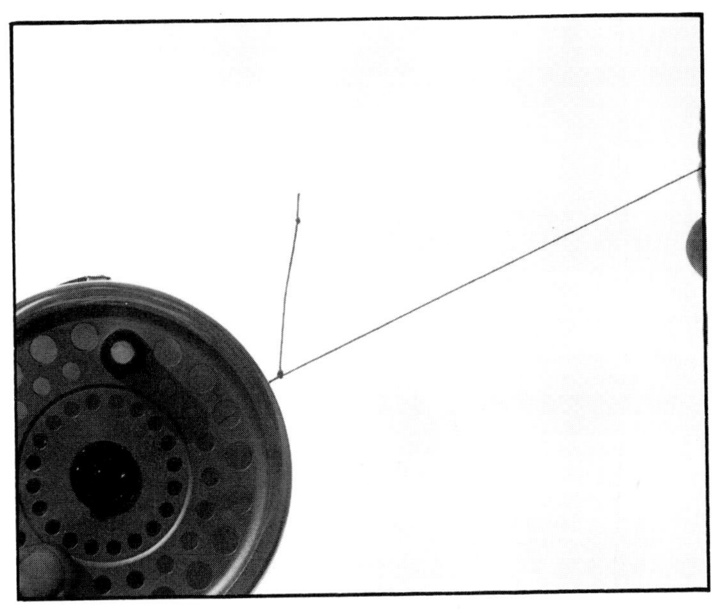

4. Pull on the standing part of the line to slide the overhand knot securely against the hub of the reel. Then, continue pulling until the overhand knot you made in the tip of the tag end slips down and jams against the other overhand knot.

5. Trim the tag end and you're ready to spool line on the reel.

Joining Lines Together

BLOOD KNOT—*Breaking strength 90%–95%*

The Blood Knot is one of the best known and most popular knots in use among fishermen today. It is the standard knot for making tapered leaders and offers the advantage of connecting lines of dissimilar size without an offset. The Blood Knot is particularly advantageous when tying very light leader tippets such as 5X, 6X, 7X, and even 8X. Basically, the Blood Knot enables you to tie together two lines with equal or unequal diameters. If the diameters of the two lines vary greatly, then we recommend the Improved Blood Knot which we shall illustrate next. But first, you should learn the basic Blood Knot.

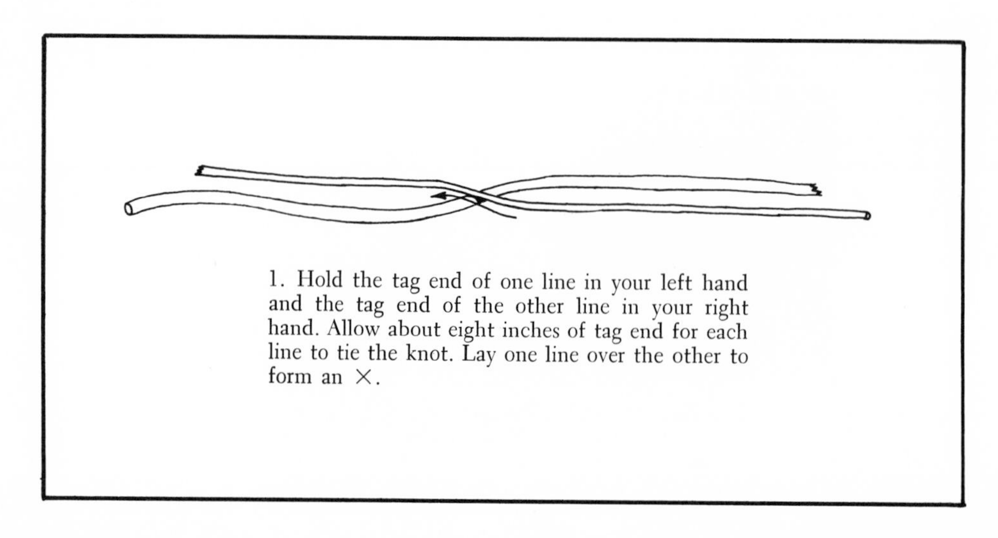

1. Hold the tag end of one line in your left hand and the tag end of the other line in your right hand. Allow about eight inches of tag end for each line to tie the knot. Lay one line over the other to form an X.

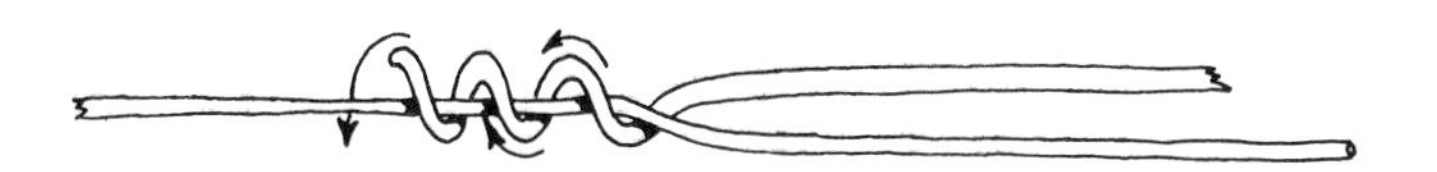

2. With your right thumb and forefinger squeeze the two lines together at the point where they cross. Using your left hand, make *five turns* with the tag end of the line extending on that side around the standing part of the other line.

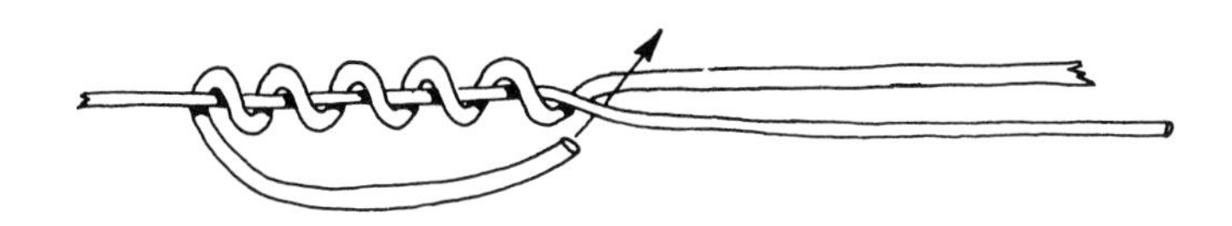

3. Now bring the tag end back toward the point where the two lines were originally crossed and insert it on the other side of the × between the other tag end and standing part. Change your grip on this spot and use your left hand to hold the knot in place.

4. Using your right hand, take five turns with the other tag end around the standing part of the other line. Assuming the lines are of fairly equal diameter, you should have five turns on each side of the ×.

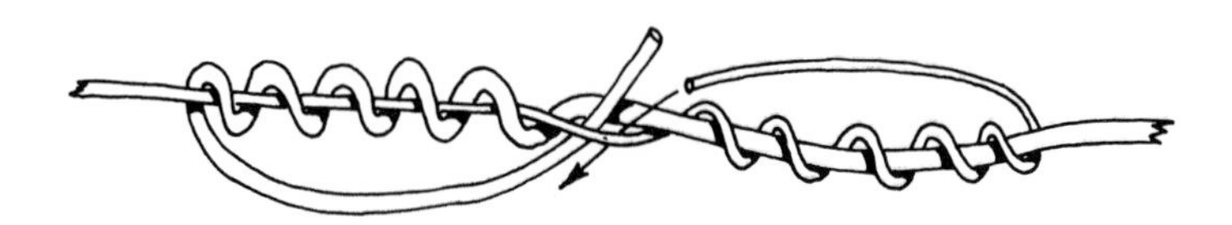

5. Now insert the second tag end through the same opening in the twists that the first tag end passed through. Two things are critical at this stage. Both tag ends must pass through the same opening with one going from bottom to top and the other from top to bottom. Studying the illustration carefully will help you to understand this concept.

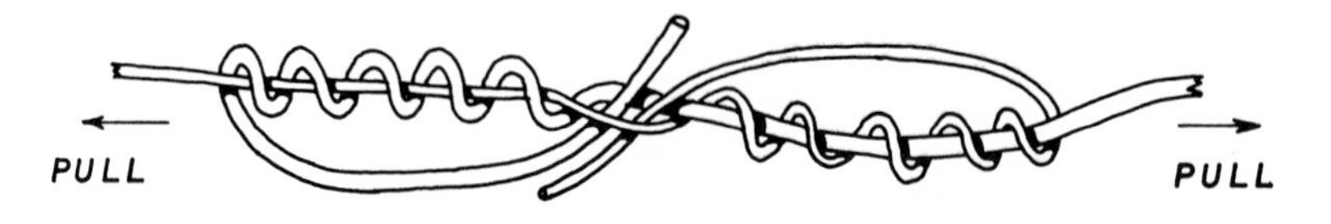

6. Take a close look at this illustration. This is the way the knot should look just before tightening. How you tighten a Blood Knot is important. Wet it first with saliva or water. Then hold one standing part in your left hand and the other in your right hand. If the breaking strength of the line or leader material is ten-pound test or stronger, the Blood Knot should be tightened by *jerking* the two standing parts. With very light tests, you'll have to pull steadily. The jerk is very important on heavier lines because it helps the turns to seat correctly.

7. All that remains to be done is the trimming of the two short tag ends and the finished knot looks like this. If you intend to use a dropper fly, see the section on creating a dropper-fly rig from a Blood Knot.

IMPROVED BLOOD KNOT—*Breaking strength 90%–100%*

When you must join lines of greatly unequal diameters and you want to use a Blood Knot, you should tie the Improved version. Remember, of course, that there are other methods available for this type of connection. The difficulty with the Improved Blood Knot is in tightening. Unless the turns are pulled up snugly, the knot will lose strength. And when you are dealing with heavier breaking strengths, it is not always easy to tighten the knot with a single jerk or pull.

To use the Improved Blood Knot effectively, you must understand the principles involved. Basically, the lighter line will tighten easily and neatly, but the heavier line might not tighten completely. For that reason, you must vary the number of turns with each line and this becomes a matter of judgment and experience. If one of the lines is twenty-pound test or under, it should be doubled if you intend to tie it to very heavy line such as sixty- or eighty-pound test.

In tying twelve-pound test to eighty-pound test, for example, you would double the twelve pound and then take seven turns against three turns with the eighty-pound test. The formula varies with the degree of dissimilarity in breaking strengths. Just remember the rule that you *take more turns with the lighter line than you do with the heavier.* A little experimentation will help you achieve the right formula for each situation.

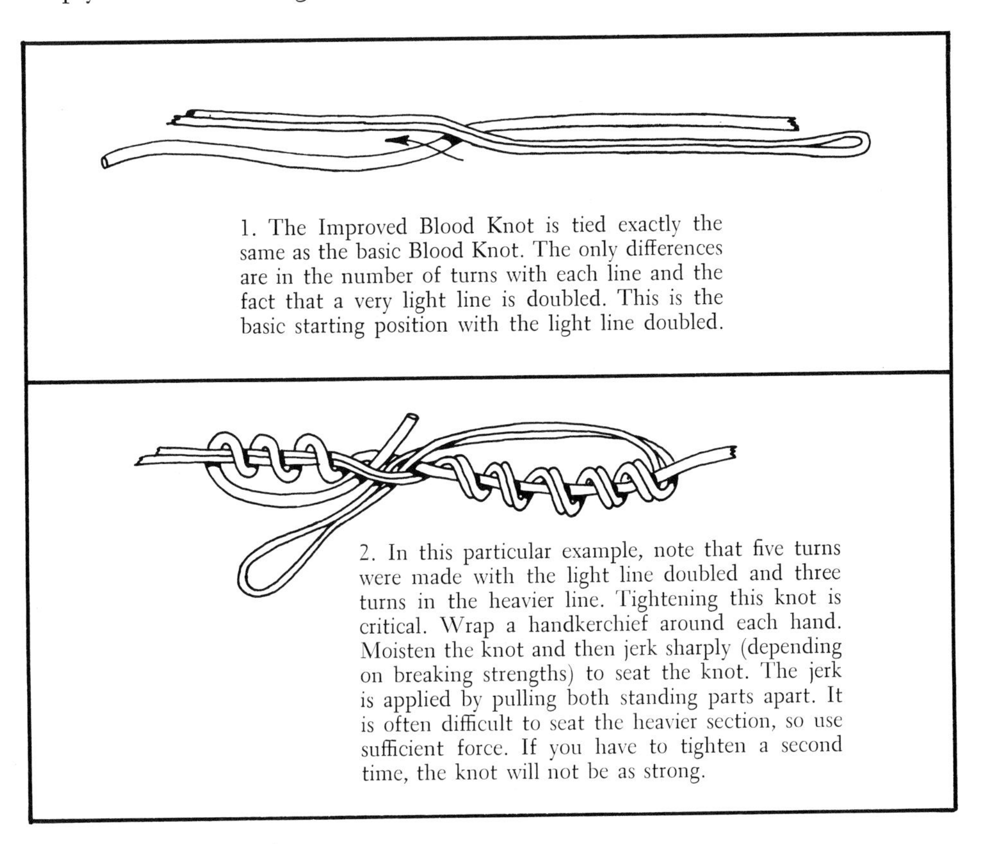

1. The Improved Blood Knot is tied exactly the same as the basic Blood Knot. The only differences are in the number of turns with each line and the fact that a very light line is doubled. This is the basic starting position with the light line doubled.

2. In this particular example, note that five turns were made with the light line doubled and three turns in the heavier line. Tightening this knot is critical. Wrap a handkerchief around each hand. Moisten the knot and then jerk sharply (depending on breaking strengths) to seat the knot. The jerk is applied by pulling both standing parts apart. It is often difficult to seat the heavier section, so use sufficient force. If you have to tighten a second time, the knot will not be as strong.

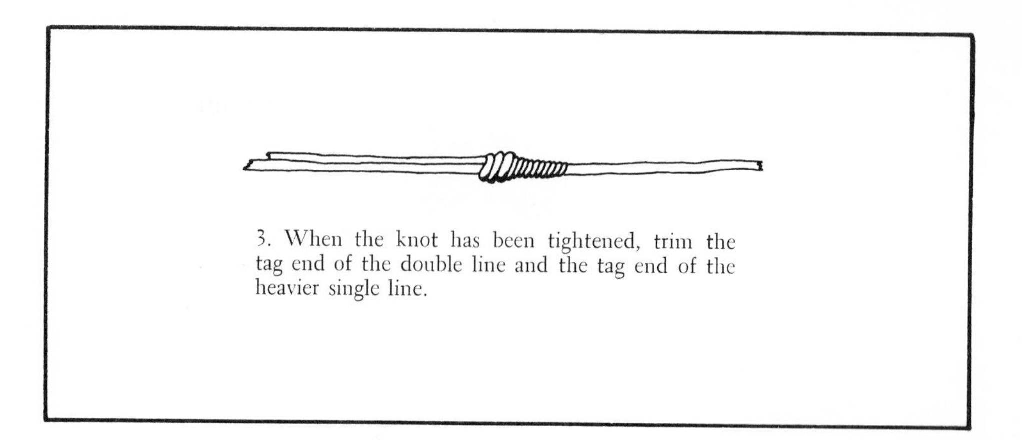

3. When the knot has been tightened, trim the tag end of the double line and the tag end of the heavier single line.

SURGEON'S KNOT—*Breaking strength 95%+*

The Surgeon's Knot is one of the quickest, easiest, and strongest knots for joining two lines of dissimilar (or similar) diameters; it will work best when the breaking strength of the heavier line is no more than four or five times that of the lighter line. If you use a Bimini Twist in the lighter line, you can count on 100% breaking strength in the Surgeon's Knot. We use this knot primarily to attach a shock tippet to the line. It's a good one and you should know it.

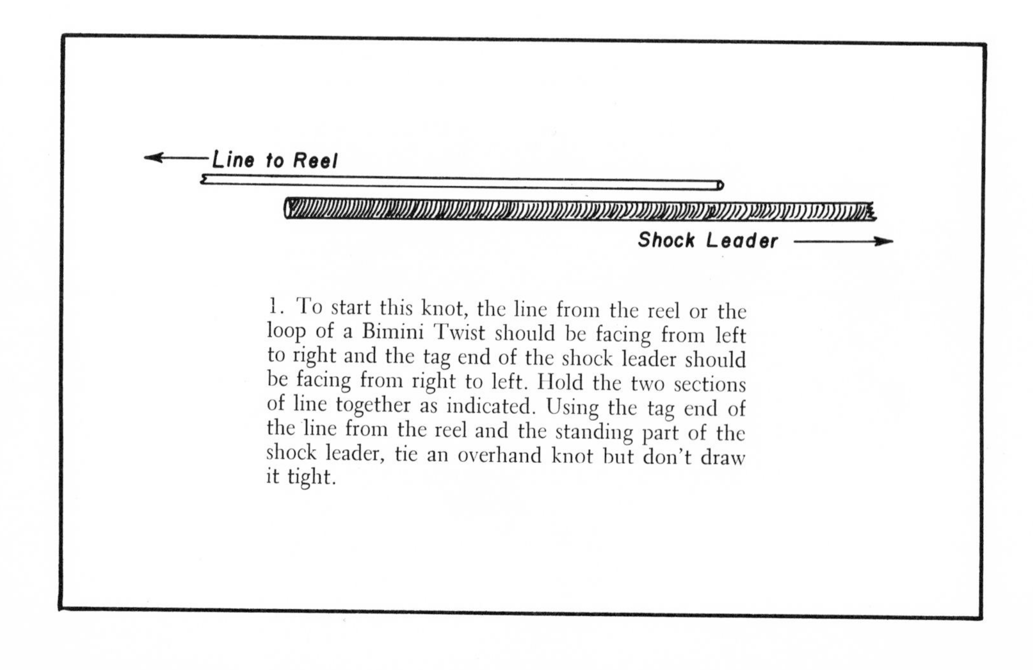

1. To start this knot, the line from the reel or the loop of a Bimini Twist should be facing from left to right and the tag end of the shock leader should be facing from right to left. Hold the two sections of line together as indicated. Using the tag end of the line from the reel and the standing part of the shock leader, tie an overhand knot but don't draw it tight.

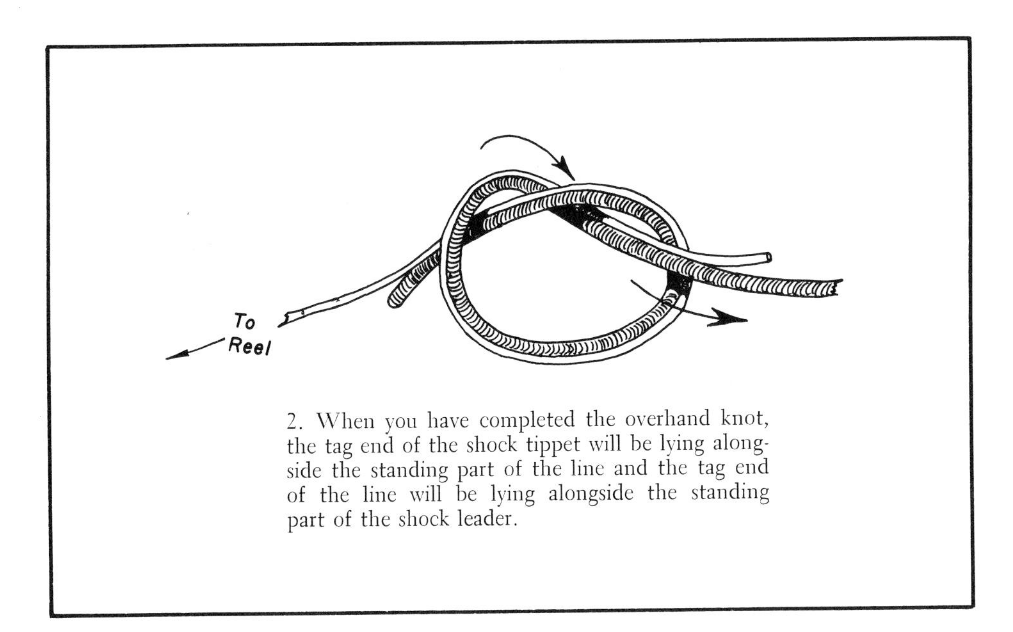

2. When you have completed the overhand knot, the tag end of the shock tippet will be lying alongside the standing part of the line and the tag end of the line will be lying alongside the standing part of the shock leader.

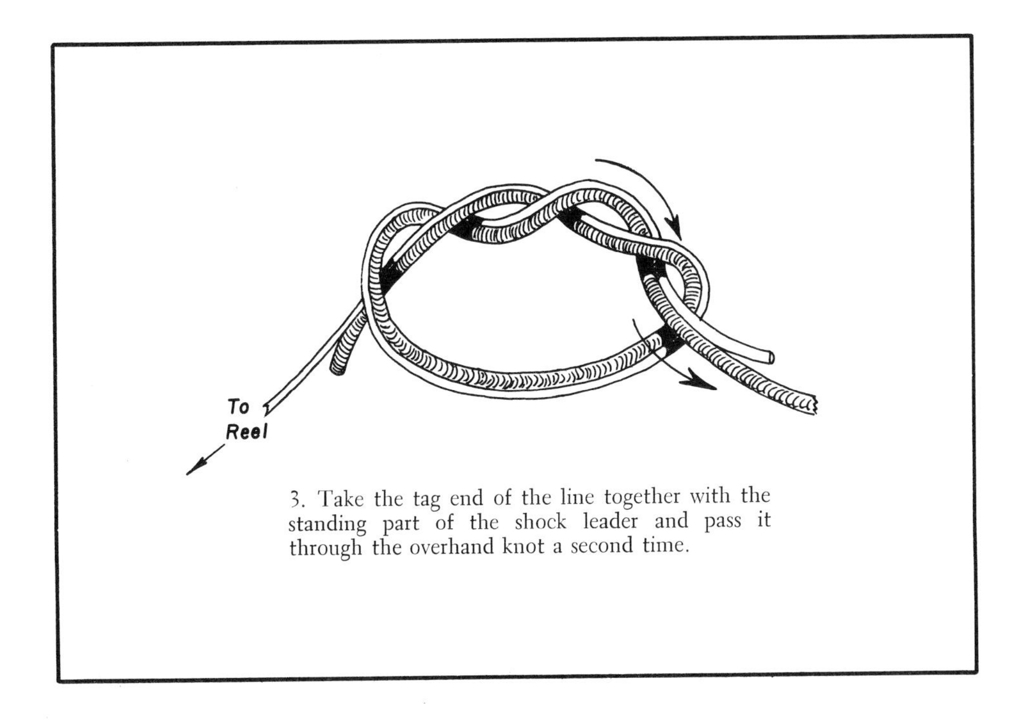

3. Take the tag end of the line together with the standing part of the shock leader and pass it through the overhand knot a second time.

4. Moisten the knot prior to tightening. Now grip the standing part of the line together with the tag end of the shock leader in your left hand. Grip the tag end of the line together with the standing part of the shock leader in your right hand. *Pull all four lines apart steadily—two on each side of the knot—to tighten.*

5. Trim the tag ends on the finished knot and you're ready to use it.

ALBRIGHT KNOT—*Connecting monofilament to monofilament*

The Albright Knot is one of the most useful knots for joining together monofilament lines of greatly unequal diameters. It is used basically for creating shock leaders and, when a Bimini Twist is tied in the end of the lighter casting line, the knot system has 100% breaking strength. For clarity in the illustrations, we are using a single strand of monofilament in the lighter breaking strength. Normally, this would be the loop end of a Bimini Twist.

1. Bend a loop in the tag end of the heavier monofilament and hold the loop between the thumb and forefinger of your left hand. Insert the tag end of the lighter monofilament through the loop. The knot is now tied identically to the Albright connecting monofilament to wire.

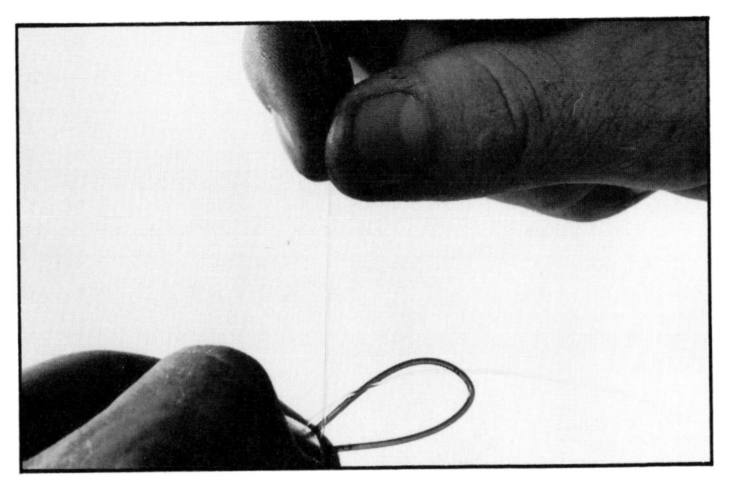

2. Slip the tag end of the lighter monofilament under your left thumb and pinch it tightly against the heavier strands of the loop. Wrap the first turn of the lighter monofilament over itself and continue wrapping toward the round end of the loop. You must take at least twelve turns with the lighter monofilament around all three strands.

3. After you have completed at least twelve turns, insert the tag end of the lighter monofilament through the end of the loop. *Remember that the monofilament must enter and leave the loop on the same side of the loop.*

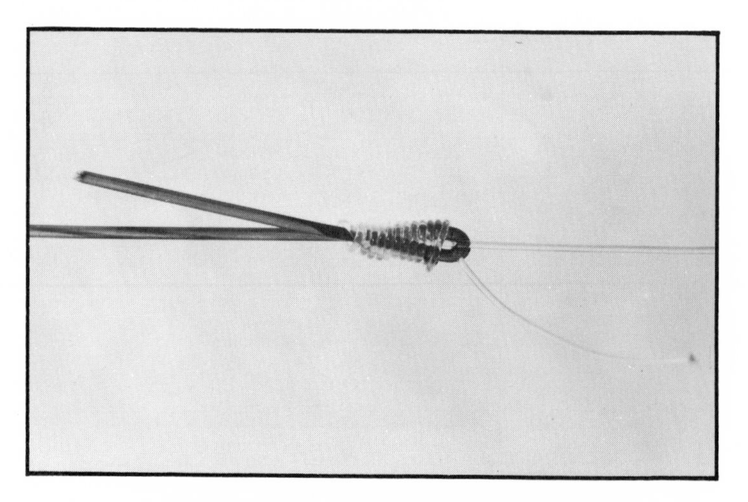

4. With the thumb and forefinger of the left hand, slide the coils of lighter monofilament together and toward the end of the heavy monofilament loop, stopping within ⅛ inch of the end.

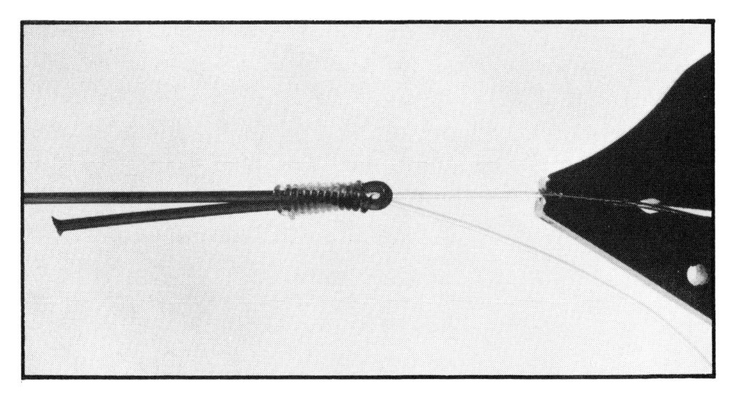

5. Using pliers for a better grip, pull the tag end of the lighter monofilament tight. *This must be done first or the coils will slip off the loop.* Your left hand should still be holding *both* strands of the heavier monofilament.

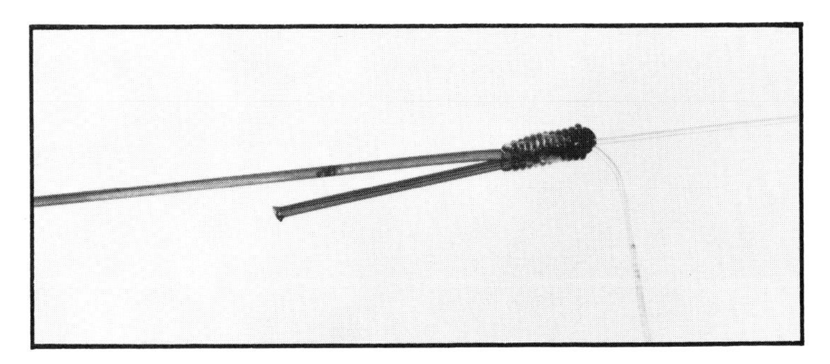

6. With your left hand still holding both the standing part and tag end of the *heavier* monofilament, pull on the standing part of the lighter monofilament. Then, pull the tag end of the lighter monofilament a second time and the standing part of the monofilament once more. Now shift your left hand to only the standing part of the heavy monofilament (releasing the tag end of the heavy mono). Pull the standing part of the heavy mono and the standing part of the light mono. If the knot is going to fail, it should pull apart in your hands.

7. Trim both tag ends closely and the finished knot will make a neat and effective connection.

ALBRIGHT KNOT (2)—*Connecting monofilament to wire*

Almost any fisherman will tell you that you cannot tie monofilament to solid wire with 100% strength in the knot. In fact, everyone knows that the wire will knife through the monofilament. Contrary to the opinions of most fishermen, it can be done and the Albright Knot is the way to do it providing you tie a Bimini Twist in the end of the casting or trolling line. Then, tie a heavier piece of monofilament to the Bimini (you only need a very short length). As an example, if you are using twelve-pound test monofilament, tie in a short length of thirty-pound test and you're ready to connect to the wire without the use of a swivel. Most of the top fishermen, by the way, avoid the use of swivels whenever they can.

1. Use a Haywire Twist to form a loop in the wire. Then, squeeze the loop into an elongated position. If you don't use a Haywire Twist, you run the risk of having the wire snake out of the knot under pressure.

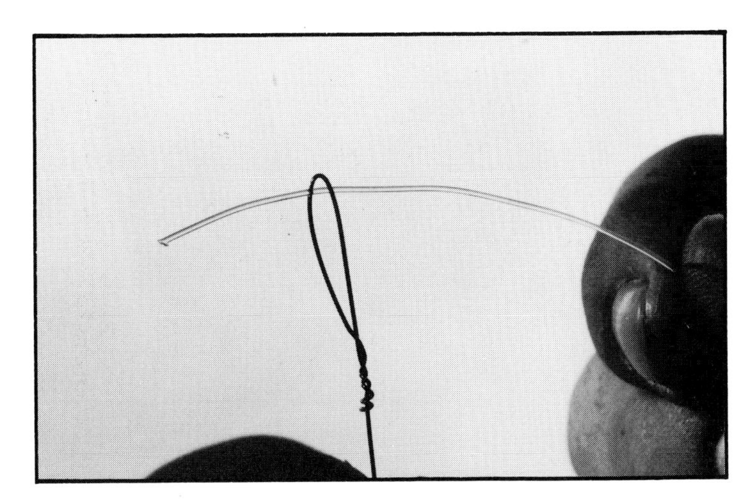

2. Insert the tag end of the monofilament through the loop in the wire, working from right to left or from bottom to top. It will take twelve to fifteen inches of monofilament to tie this knot.

3. The monofilament will be lying alongside the wire with the tag end of the mono pointing toward the standing part of the wire. Take the tag end of the monofilament in your right hand and hold both strands of the wire loop plus the monofilament passing through the loop in your left hand. Remember that *all* wraps with the monofilament will be made *toward the round end of the wire loop* (and toward the standing part of the monofilament). The first wrap is the most difficult because you must wrap back over the monofilament. Once you get the first turn or two, pinch the turns with thumb and forefinger of your left hand and continue to wrap the tag end of the monofilament over the two sections of wire in the loop and the standing part of the monofilament. You will need at least ten wraps.

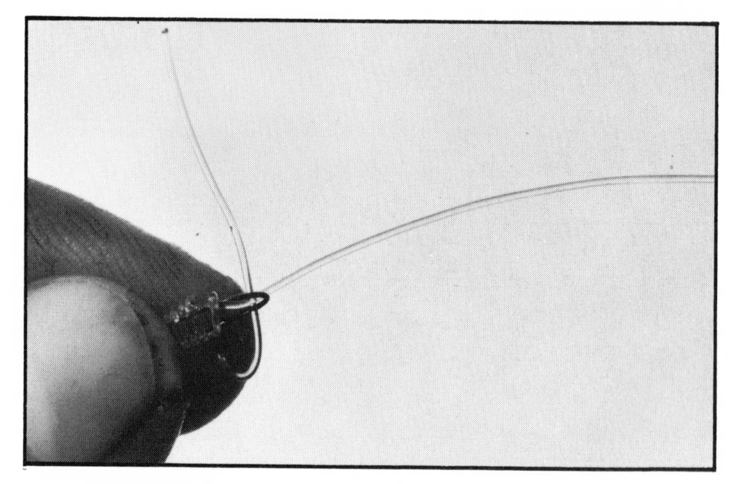

4. Tension must be maintained on the tag end and the turns should be pinched with the fingers of the left hand as they are taken. After you have made ten turns with the mono, push the tag end of the monofilament through the end of the wire loop. The tag end of the monofilament *must come out of the wire loop in the same direction it originally entered.* If you inserted the mono from bottom to top, then the tag end goes out from top to bottom. If you pushed it in from right to left, it exits left to right.

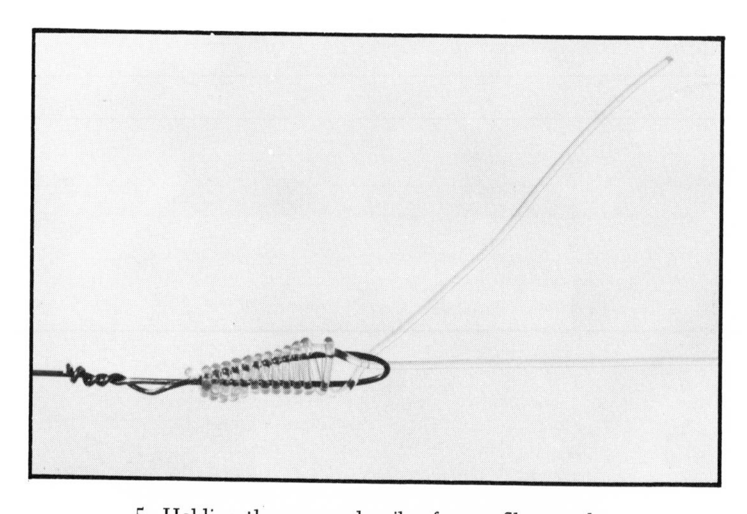

5. Holding the wrapped coils of monofilament between the thumb and forefinger of the left hand, push the coils together and within 1/8 inch from the end of the loop. Be careful not to push the coils too far or they will slide over the loop and the knot will come apart.

6. The Albright Knot is tightened in stages. Grip the tag end of the monofilament with pliers and pull it tight *first,* while you hold the standing part of the wire with your other hand. *The short end of the mono must be tightened first or the knot will slip over the wire loop.* Then pull on the standing part of the monofilament. Another pull on the tag end of the monofilament and a second pull on the standing part of the monofilament should tighten the knot securely. Test it by pulling on the standing part of the wire and the standing part of the monofilament.

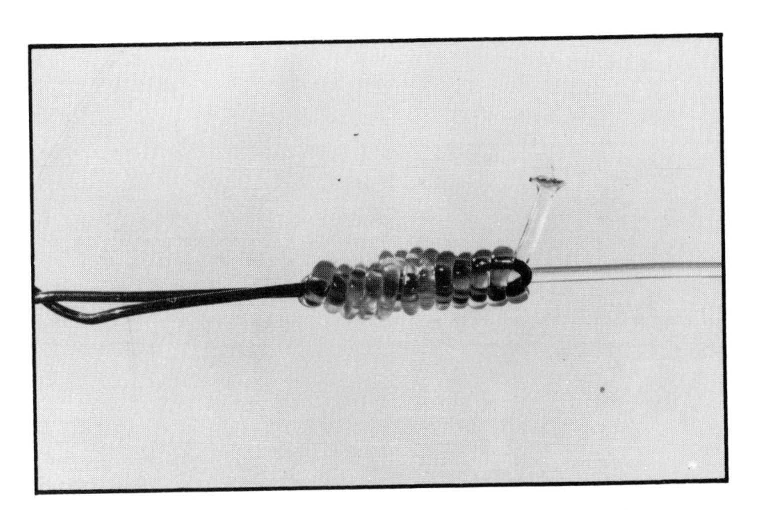

7. The knot is only drawn tight when the coils of monofilament are jammed against the tag end. This is a jam knot and must be tightened correctly or it will eventually come apart. We have purposely trimmed the tag end longer than usual so you will be able to study the principle of the knot. Normally, the tag end would be trimmed close to avoid hanging up in rod guides or the tip-top.

JOINING LEAD CORE TO MONOFILAMENT OR DACRON
(Modified Nail Knot)

This knot was originally developed for trollers who used lead-core line to fish deep, but, in recent years, it has also become an important tool of the fly-fisherman. Some fly rodders are now using a lead-core shooting head to fish deeper and they have had a problem connecting monofilament shooting line or Dacron backing to the lead core. The knot is really a Modified Nail Knot and before you start, take a moment or two to study the procedure outlined under Nail Knot.

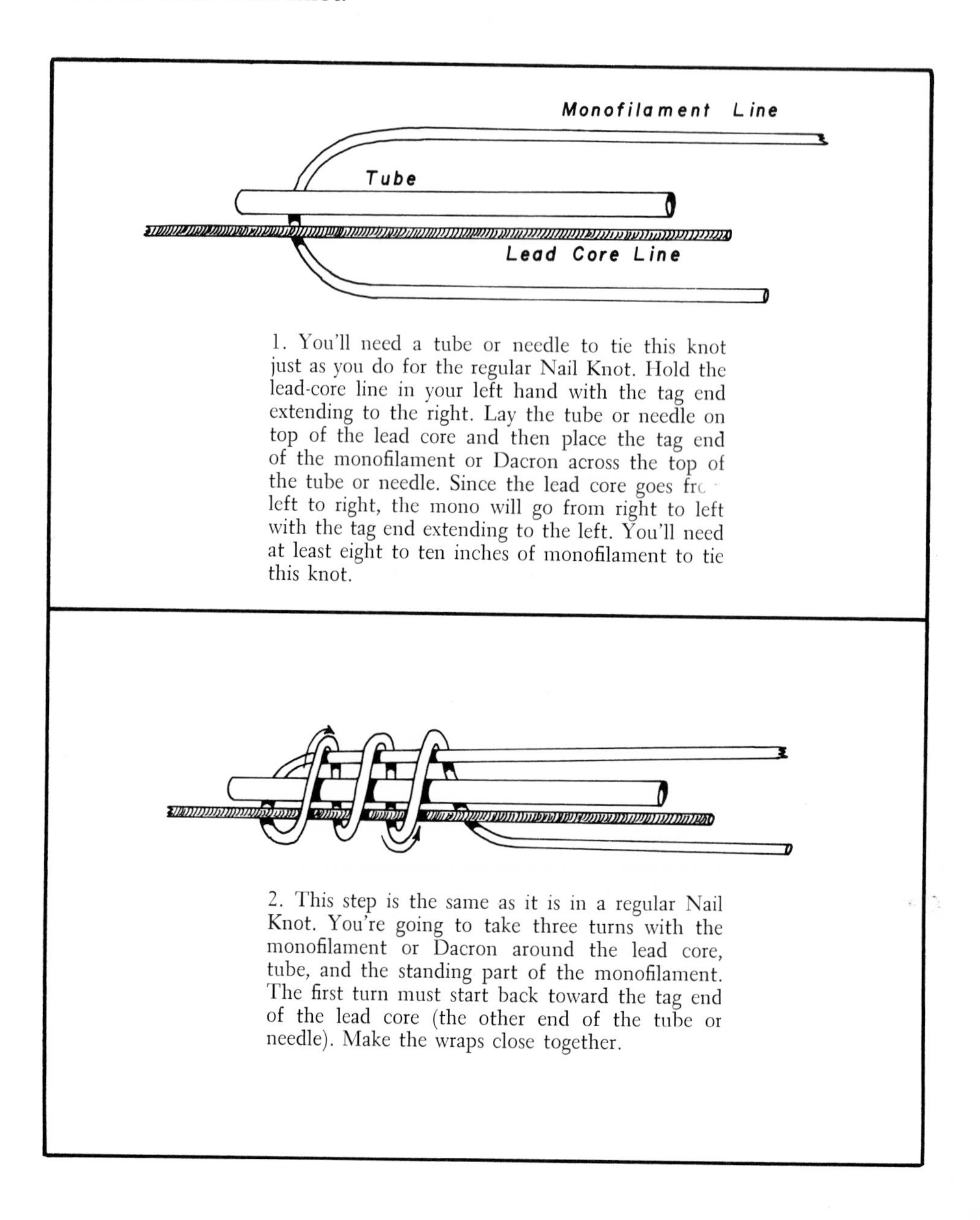

1. You'll need a tube or needle to tie this knot just as you do for the regular Nail Knot. Hold the lead-core line in your left hand with the tag end extending to the right. Lay the tube or needle on top of the lead core and then place the tag end of the monofilament or Dacron across the top of the tube or needle. Since the lead core goes from left to right, the mono will go from right to left with the tag end extending to the left. You'll need at least eight to ten inches of monofilament to tie this knot.

2. This step is the same as it is in a regular Nail Knot. You're going to take three turns with the monofilament or Dacron around the lead core, tube, and the standing part of the monofilament. The first turn must start back toward the tag end of the lead core (the other end of the tube or needle). Make the wraps close together.

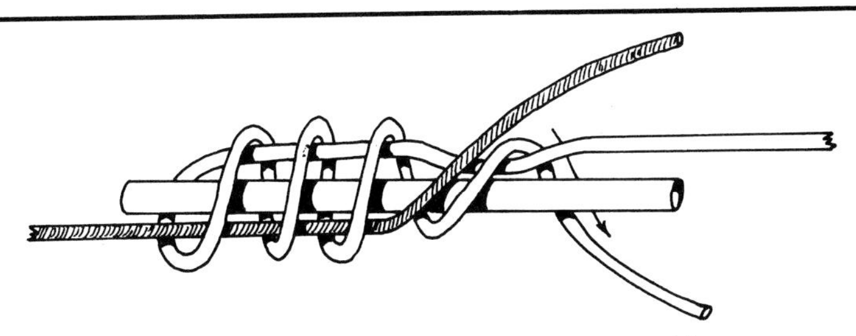

3. After you have made the first three turns with the tag end of the monofilament around the tube, lead core, and standing part of the monofilament, lift the tag end of the lead core up and out of the way. Now make one turn with the monofilament around the standing part of the monofilament and the tube.

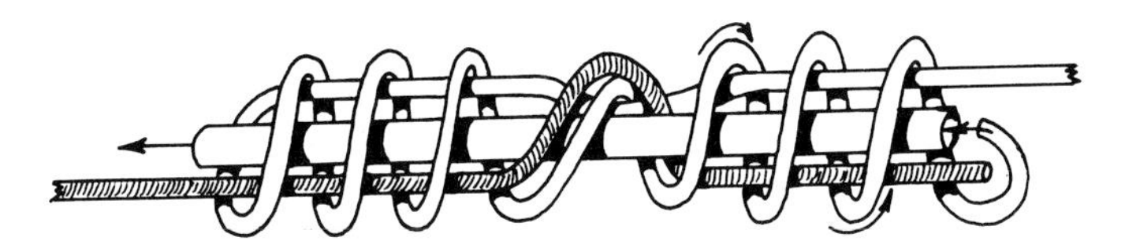

4. Place the lead core back against the tube and take three more turns with the monofilament around the lead core, tube, and the standing part of the monofilament. The turns should be as close together as possible.

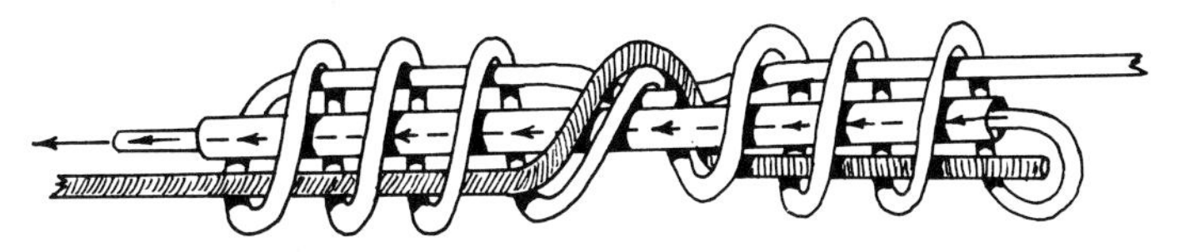

5. Insert the tag end of the monofilament through the tube or needle, working from right to left. The tag end must pass through all of the wraps. Then, slowly extract the tube, pulling the monofilament through with it. The tube is extracted to your left or toward the standing part of the lead core.

6. Hold the knot securely so that the turns do not unravel. Pull on the tag end of the monofilament and then the standing part of the monofilament to tighten the knot. When the knot is as tight as you can make it, test it by pulling on the standing part of the lead core and the standing part of the monofilament. Trim the tag end of the lead core and the tag end of the monofilament close to the knot.

JOINING MONEL TO BRAIDED LINE

This connection is used to join wire line to braided line for deep trolling situations. Remember that wire line should be used only on a conventional type reel and there should never be more wire on the reel than you actually need for fishing. The rest of the spool is filled with braided line.

1. A Bimini Twist is tied in the tag end of the braided line. (You could use one of the end loops such as the Double Surgeon's Loop or Improved End Loop.) Insert the wire through the loop in the braided line, leaving a tag end of about eighteen inches.

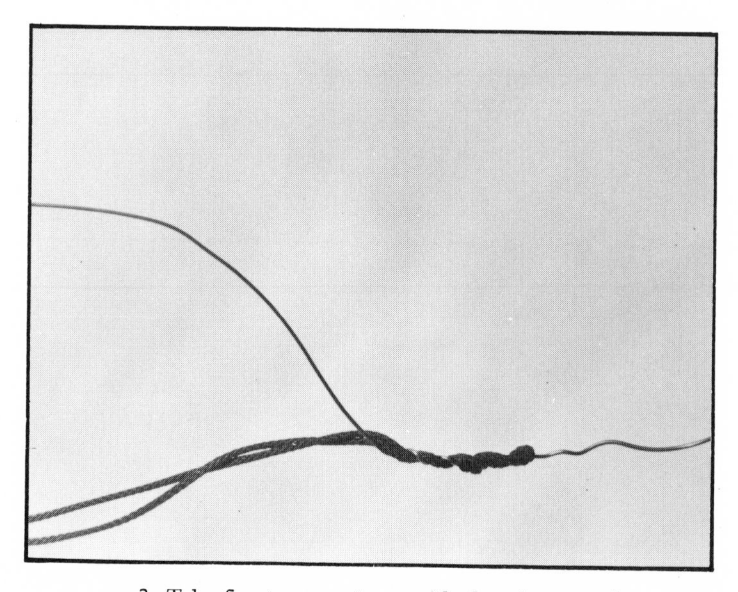

2. Take five to seven turns with the wire around *both* standing parts of the loop in the braided line.

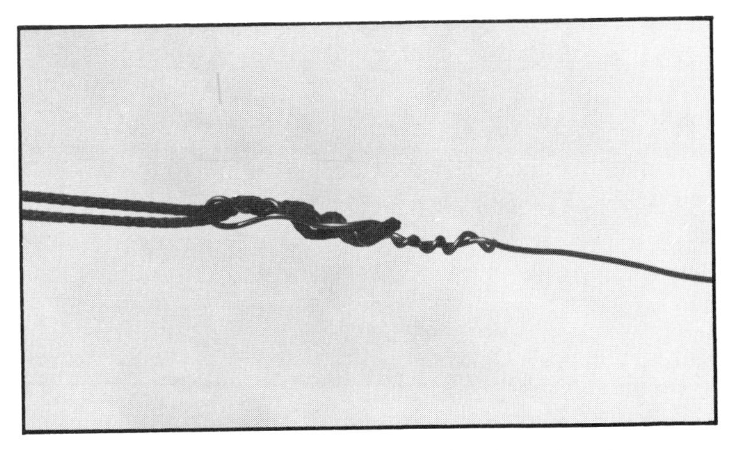

3. Now reverse the turns with the wire and work back toward the standing part of the wire line. Pass the tag end of the wire through the end of the loop in the braided line when you reach that point and finish off the knot by twisting the tag end of the wire around the standing part of the wire.

Loops

DOUBLE SURGEON'S LOOP

The Double Surgeon's Loop is a quick and easy way to tie a loop in the end of a leader. It is often used as part of a leader system because it is relatively strong.

1. Double the tag end of the line.

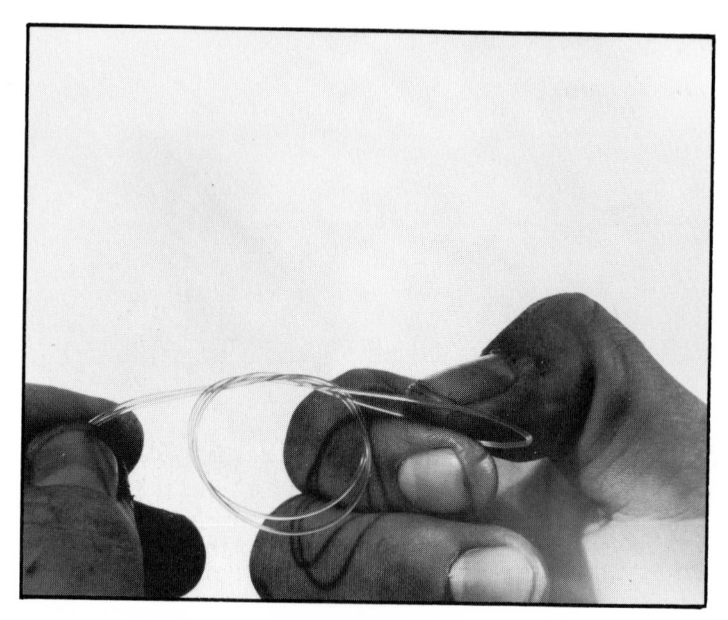

2. Make a simple overhand knot in the double line.

3. Hold the tag end and standing part of the line in your left hand and bring the loop around to insert again in the overhand knot.

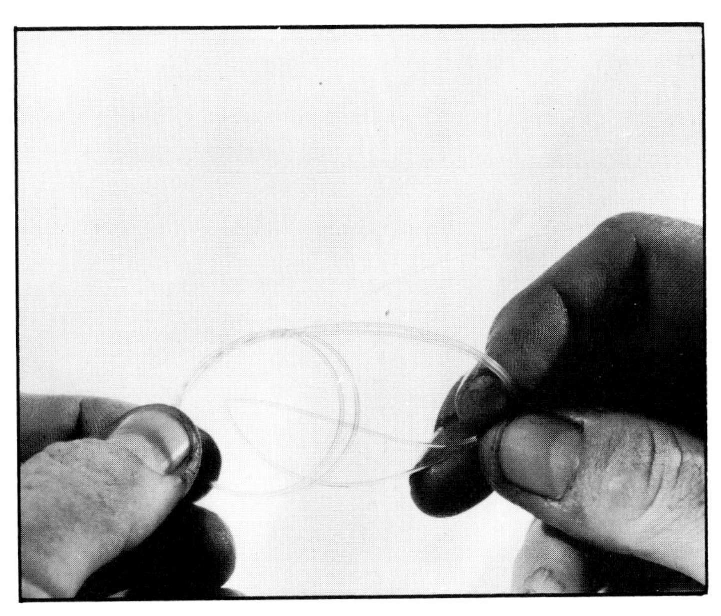

4. Insert the end of the loop in the overhand knot.

5. Hold both strands of the loop in your right hand and both the tag end and standing part in your left hand. Moisten the knot and pull your hands apart, tightening the knot.

6. Trim off the tag end close to the knot and the finished product is a neat, quickly tied loop.

PERFECTION LOOP

The Perfection Loop provides a quick and easy way to put a loop in the end of a length of line. It will take a little practice before you can tie this knot with any speed, but once you learn the method, you can tie it in a matter of seconds. Commercially snelled hooks usually have a Perfection Loop in the other end.

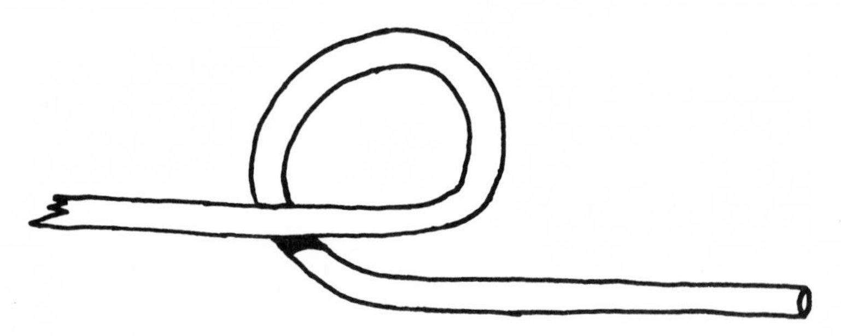

1. Hold the leader about six inches in from the tag end between the thumb and forefinger of your right hand. Leave a gap of about another six inches and hold the standing part between the thumb and forefinger of your left hand. Make a loop by passing the tag end under the standing part. To do this, turn your right hand under your left hand and the loop will form. Slide the loop under your left thumb and hold it securely.

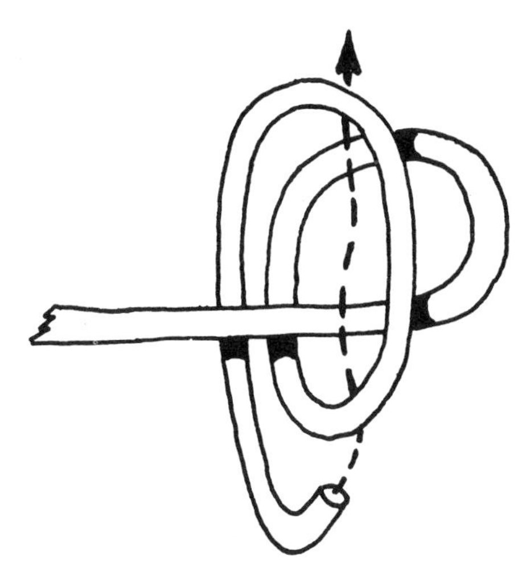

2. You can release your grip on the tag end with your right hand because the loop is being held under your left thumb. Take the tag end and make a second *loose* loop over your left thumb and around the first loop, sliding the tag end under the first loop between the thumb and forefinger of your left hand. Your left hand is now holding both loops and you can again let go of the tag end.

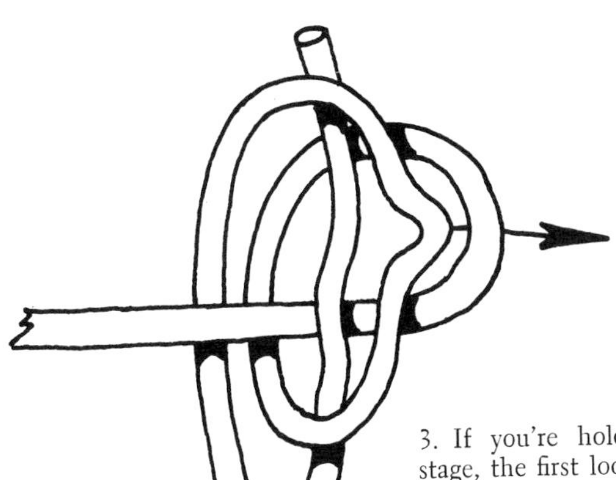

3. If you're holding the knot correctly at this stage, the first loop is pinched between the thumb and forefinger of your left hand and the second loop passes loosely over your thumb and then under the first loop. That, too, is gripped with the thumb and forefinger of your left hand. The tag end extends to the right as you face the knot, coming out from under the thumb and forefinger. If you've reached this stage, the rest is easy. Take the tag end in your right hand and bend it 180° from right to left *between* the two loops. It will pass directly between the thumb and forefinger of your left hand. Pinch the tag end to hold it in place. Now push the second loop (the one over your thumb) through the first loop.

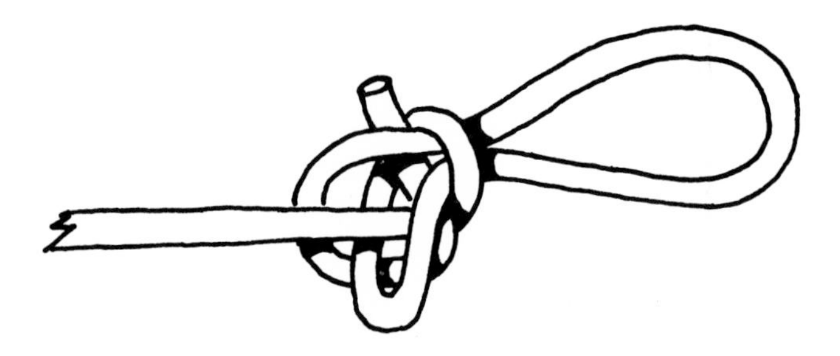

4. To tighten the knot, pull on the standing part and the second loop (the one that passed through the first loop). With heavier monofilament, insert the handle of a pair of pliers through the loop and use it to gain leverage when tightening.

DROPPER LOOP

For some smaller species of fish or for catching bait, anglers often employ several artificial lures at one time. The rig is easy to make if you follow a few basic rules. The loops must be kept short enough and far enough apart to prevent the lures from tangling. Usually, a heavy jig is tied to the end of the rig to add weight and provide a lure for larger fish if they are in the vicinity. We prefer to use the Double Surgeon's Loop for this type of rig because it is one of the quickest loops to tie and it ranks as one of the strongest. In salt water, this rig could be used for mackerel, blue runners, and other smaller fish.

Wire and Cable

FIGURE EIGHT KNOT—*Breaking strength 95%–100%*

For those anglers who prefer braided wire, the Figure Eight Knot is a quick way to tie the wire to a hook or lure.

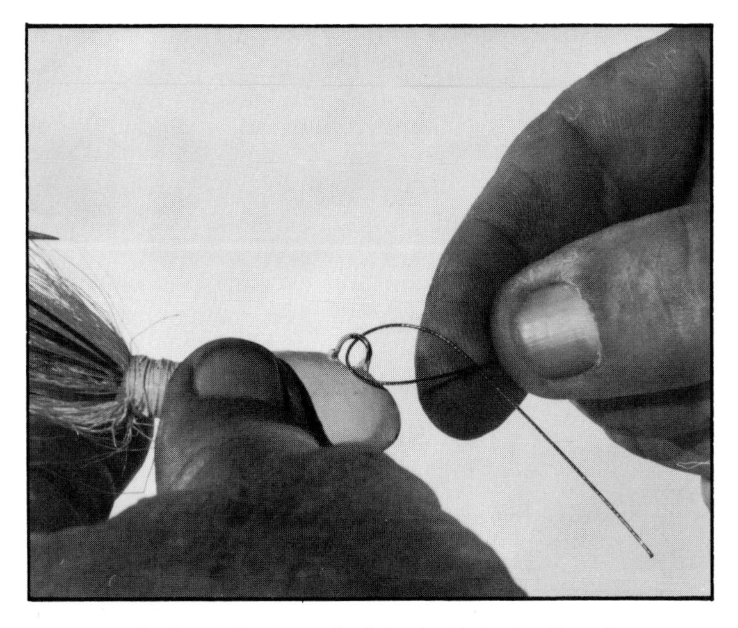

1. Insert the tag end of the braided wire through the eye of the hook or lure. Bring the tag end back and lay it under the standing part of the line.

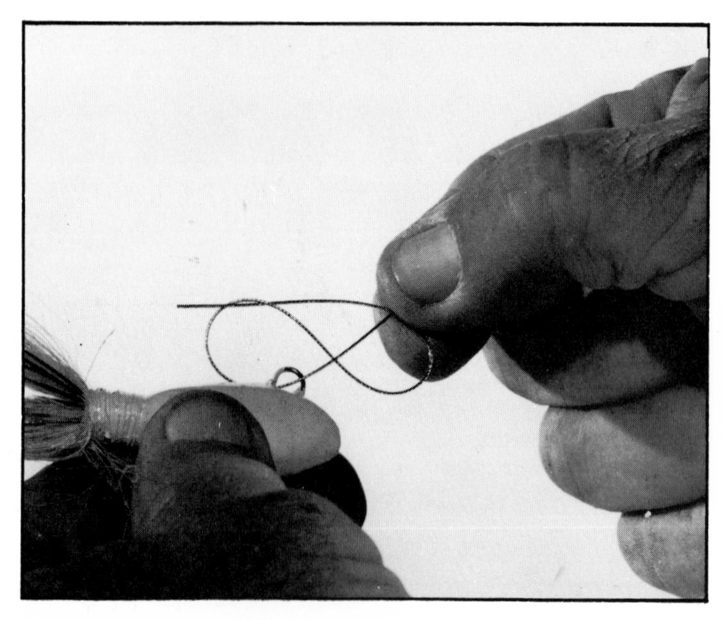

2. Pass the tag end over the standing part and insert it in the loop that is formed at the eye of the hook or lure. You are actually making a figure eight.

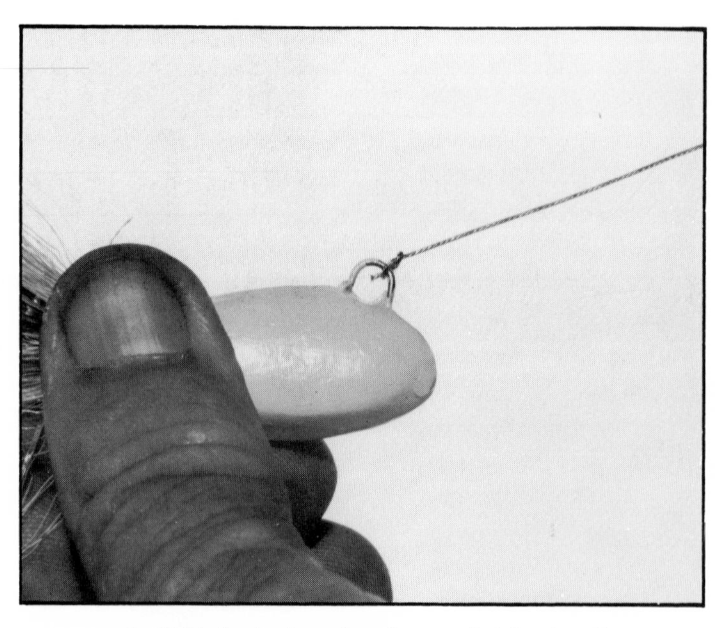

3. Hold the hook or lure in your left hand and pull the standing part of the braided wire with your right hand to seat the knot. Trim the knot leaving about 1/16 of an inch of wire extending past the tightened knot.

HEATED TWIST—*Breaking strength 95%–100%*

Instead of tying a knot in plastic-coated wire to form a loop at the end or attach it to a hook, lure, or swivel, you can fuse the plastic together with the correct application of heat. The Heated Twist is an extremely strong connection and it can be completed in a matter of seconds.

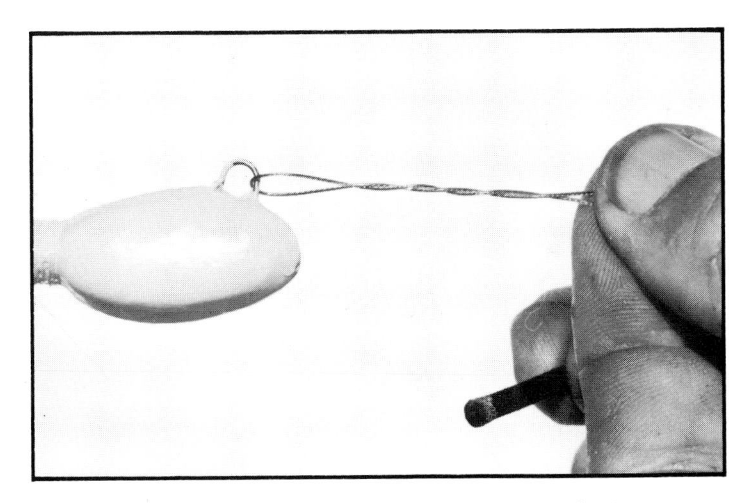

1. Insert the tag end of the plastic-coated wire through the eye of the hook or lure and make at least four twists with the tag end around the standing part. After you have completed the twists, hold the remainder of the tag end against the standing part to keep the twists from unraveling.

2. Hold a lighted match about one inch below the twists and move the match back and forth. As soon as the plastic coating over the wire begins to turn milky white, remove the match. The trick is to fuse the molecules of plastic without melting away the plastic coating and without burning it. After the fusion has cooled for several seconds, try pulling the knot apart. You'll be amazed at how strong it is.

HAYWIRE TWIST—*Breaking strength 95%–100%*

The Haywire Twist is the strongest connection for tying solid wire to a hook, lure, swivel, or for making a loop in the end of solid wire. If you do not put a Haywire Twist in wire and insist only in using a Barrel Twist (the second part of the Haywire), it could pull out under extreme pressure. This might seem unlikely to you, but it happens more frequently than most anglers suspect.

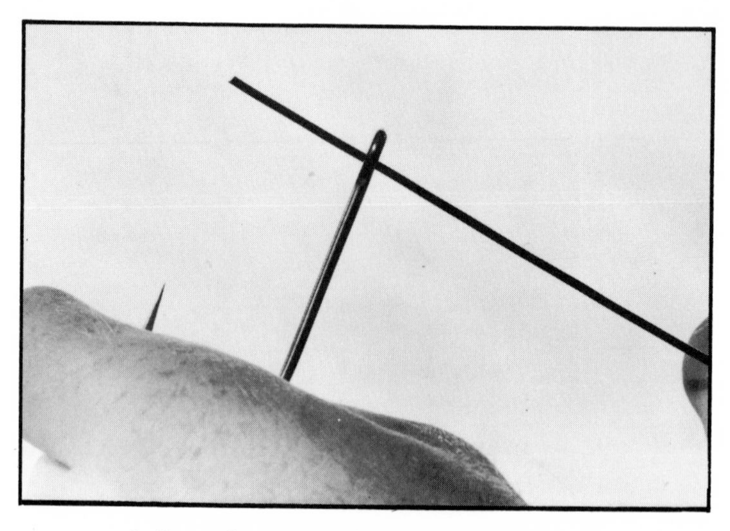

1. Insert the tag end of the wire through the eye of the hook.

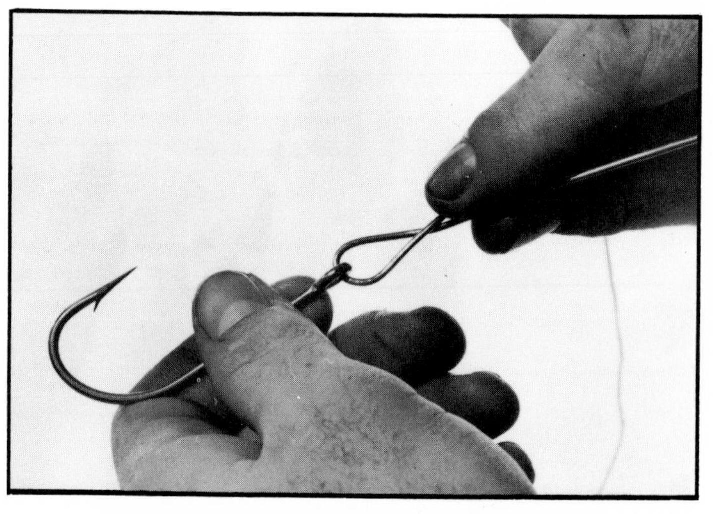

2. Bend the tag end back against the standing part of the wire forming a small loop. If you merely want to make a loop without attaching the wire to anything, this would become Step 1.

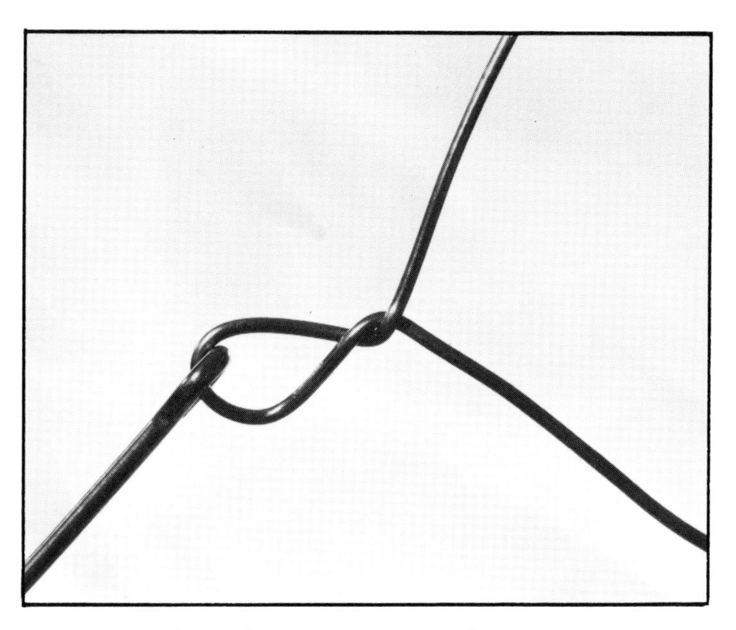

3. Grasp the loop between the thumb and forefinger of one hand and both the standing part and tag end of the wire between the thumb and forefinger of the other hand. You must *twist* both sections of wire simultaneously to form an X. Otherwise, the tag end will wrap around the standing part and you won't gain the strength of a Haywire Twist.

4. Make at least 3½ X wraps in the wire. Then, bend the tag end of wire at right angles to the standing part.

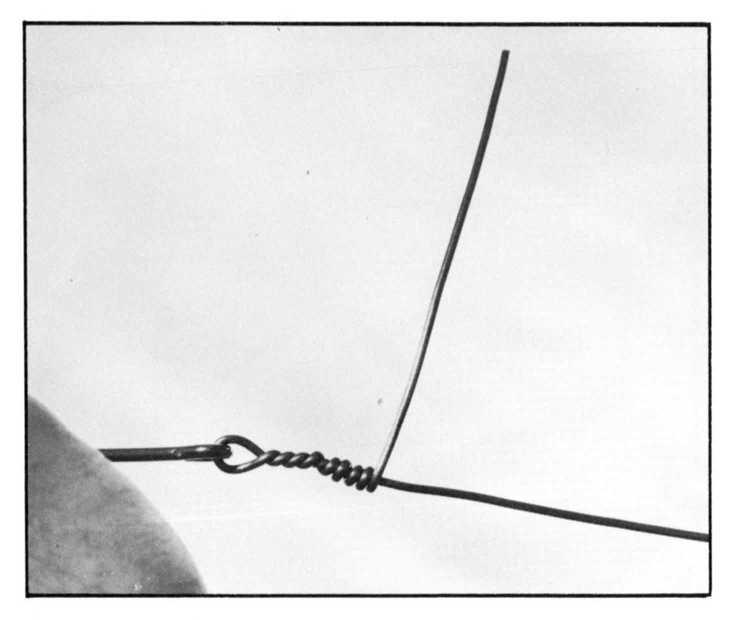

5. Hold the Haywire portion of the Twist in one hand and start a Barrel Twist by bending the tag end around the standing part in several neat, parallel coils.

6. When you have completed the barrel turns, bend the top of the tag end at right angles to form a handle for breaking the wire. This bend is made *away* from the standing part of the wire and *not* over the standing part.

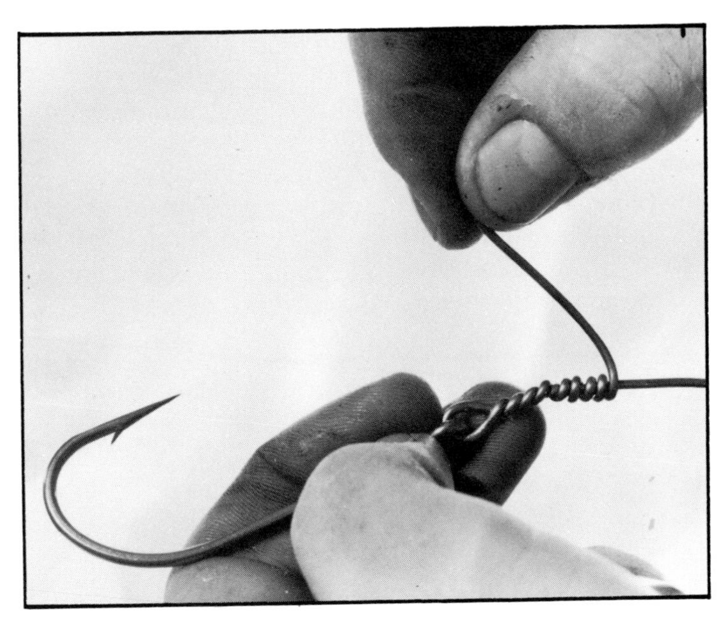

7. Hold the Haywire Twist in one hand and the handle on the tag end in the other hand. Rock the tag end back and forth until the wire breaks. Solid wire should never be cut with a tool because it will leave a sharp burr that could cause an injury.

8. The finished Twist will have at least 3½ Haywire turns in it plus a series of barrel turns.

CRIMPING CABLE—*Breaking strength 95%–100%*

The easiest way to attach multistrand wire or light cable to a hook, swivel, or lure is by crimping sleeves securely over both strands. Sleeves may also be used to form a loop in the other end of the leader. There are some anglers who use this same method with very heavy monofilament leader material because the knots are bulky and they have difficulty drawing knots tight.

The method we are illustrating incorporates a single sleeve. For extra security, you can use two sleeves about a half inch apart.

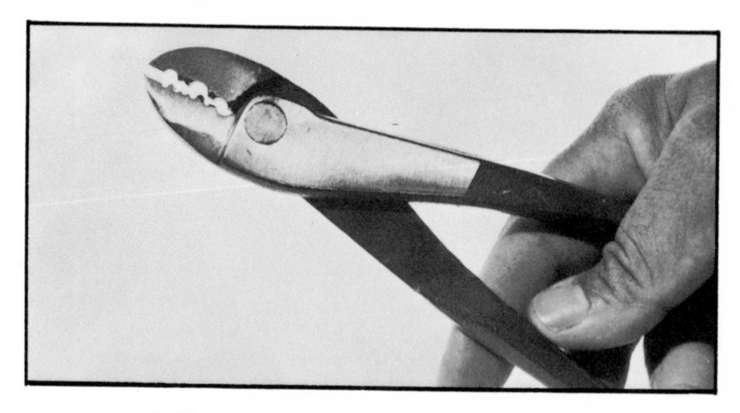

1. To crimp a sleeve properly, you should have a pair of special crimping pliers similar to the one illustrated. In an emergency, you can crimp with a pair of side-cutting pliers or regular fishing pliers, but in each case you must exercise special caution to insure that the crimp is of the correct depth without cutting through.

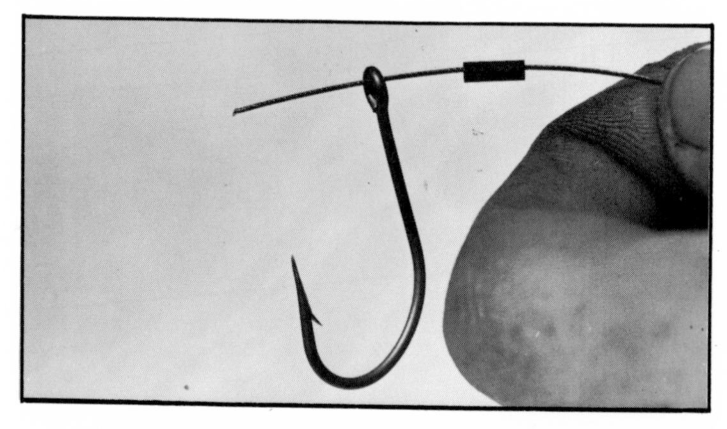

2. It is extremely important to use the proper size sleeve when crimping. Sleeve sizes are given on the package. Insert the tag end of the cable through the *proper size sleeve*. If you want a stronger connection, use two sleeves. Then, if you are attaching a hook or swivel, slip the tag end of the cable through the eye of the hook or swivel. If you are simply making a loop, this step is not necessary.

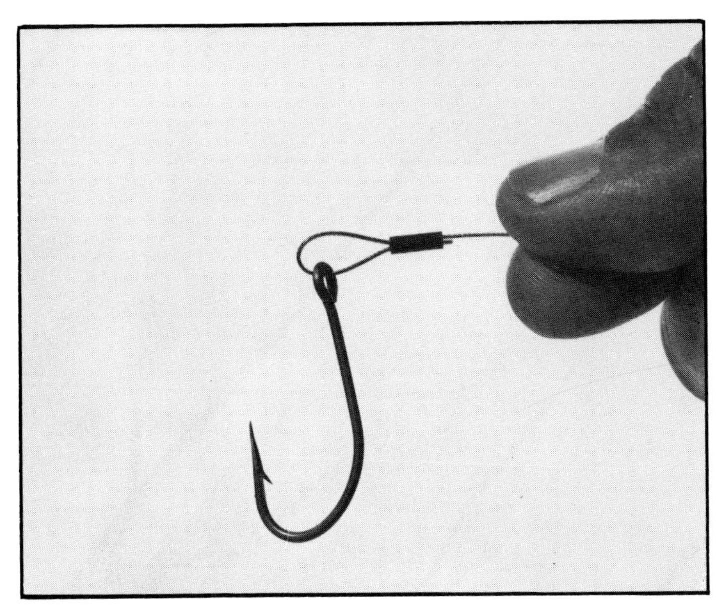

3. Push the tag end of the cable back through the sleeve or sleeves, adjusting the size of the loop.

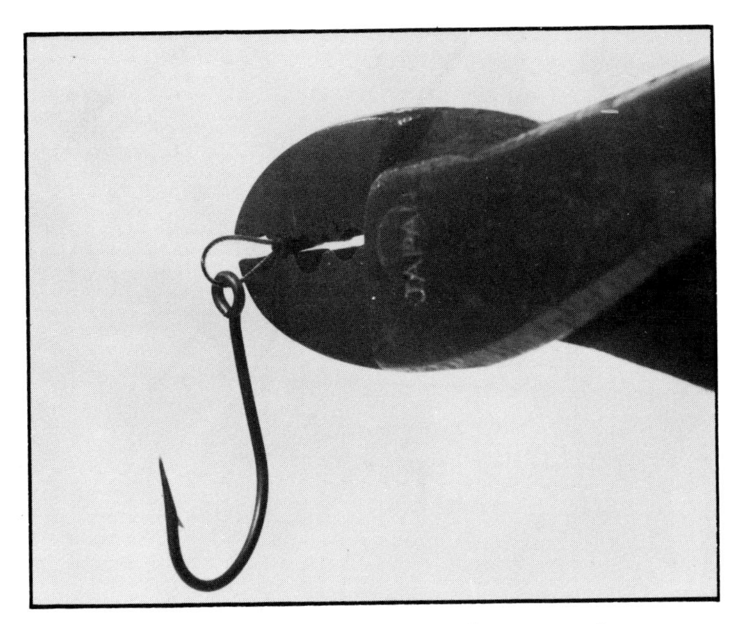

4. If you use crimping pliers, make sure to select the notch in the pliers that fits the sleeve. With the loop adjusted to the correct size, grip the head of the sleeve (the side toward the loop) with the pliers and squeeze. Do the same thing with the other end of the sleeve.

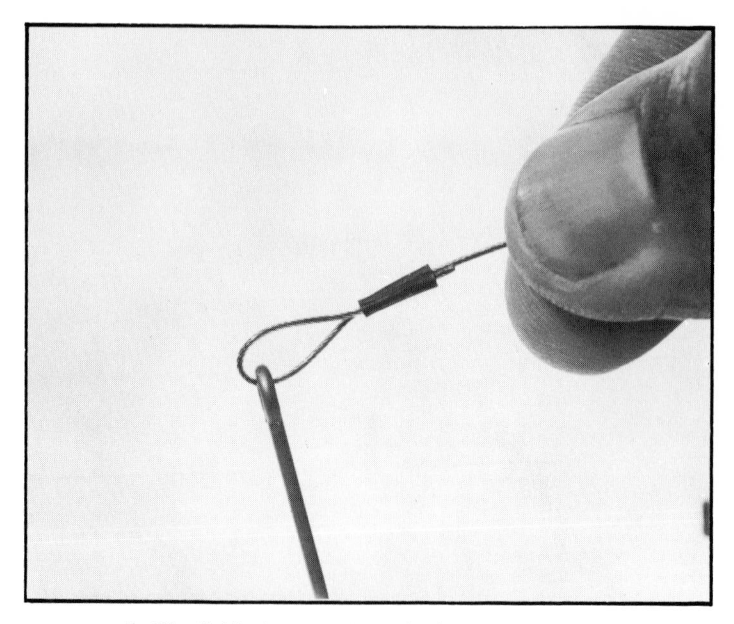

5. The finished connection is both neat and strong.

LOOPING BIG-GAME CABLE—*Breaking strength 95%–100%*

Multistrand aircraft cable is tailored for heavy duty big-game fishing and the connection must be equally strong. If you were to use a simple crimp, the cable might fray or abrade where it was bent over the eye of a hook or swivel. And, it is difficult to imagine the tremendous force that challenges the connection when a trophy fish is on the other end. For that reason, aircraft cable should be carefully looped before you go fishing.

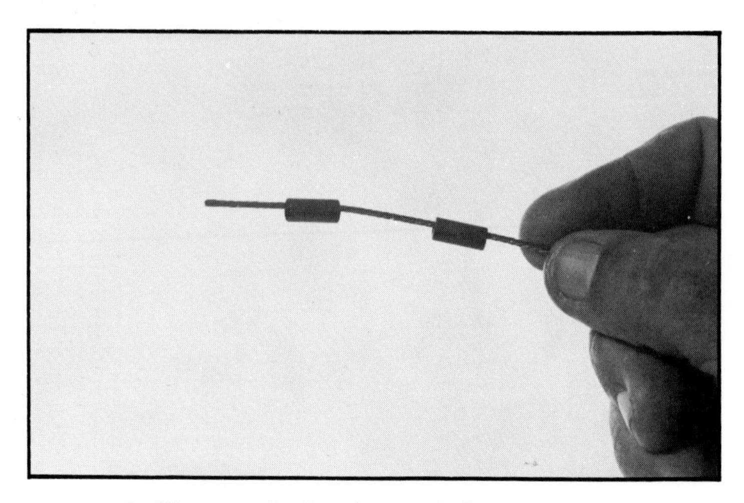

1. Slip two crimping sleeves of the *proper size* over the tag end of the cable.

2. Insert the tag end of the cable through the eye of the hook or swivel.

3. Pass the tag end of the cable through the eye of the hook or swivel a second time. Be sure to leave about a foot of the tag end to work with.

4. Hold the standing part of the cable at the hook eye and grip the loop to make sure it doesn't slide. Then, slip the tag end of the cable through the loop to form an overhand knot. Do not tighten this knot.

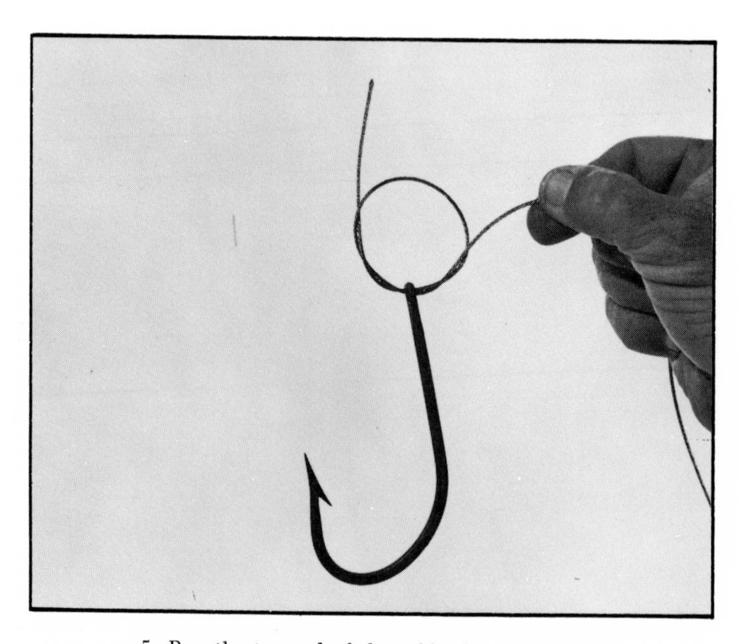

5. Pass the tag end of the cable through the loop *twice* more. That's the equivalent of forming a triple Overhand Knot.

6. Hold the tag end of the cable alongside and parallel to the standing part. Work the loop down toward the eye of the hook so that it is small and relatively tight.

7. This close up shows how the loop should look at the end of Step 6.

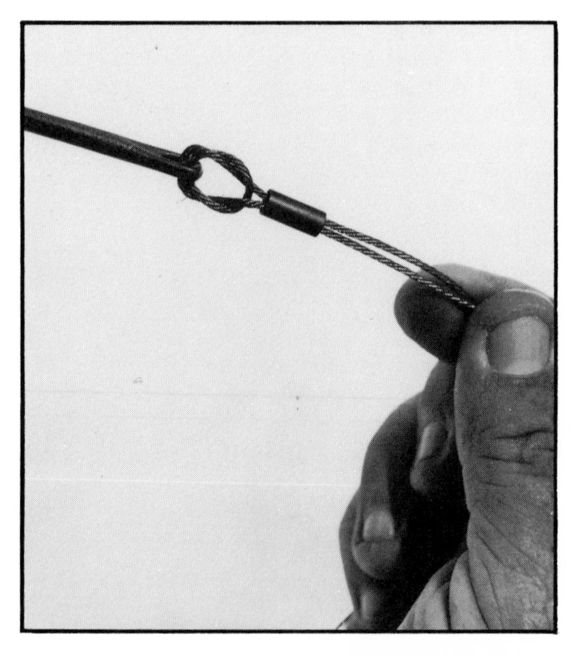

8. Slide the first sleeve over *both* parts of the cable—standing part and tag end—and seat it very close to the loop.

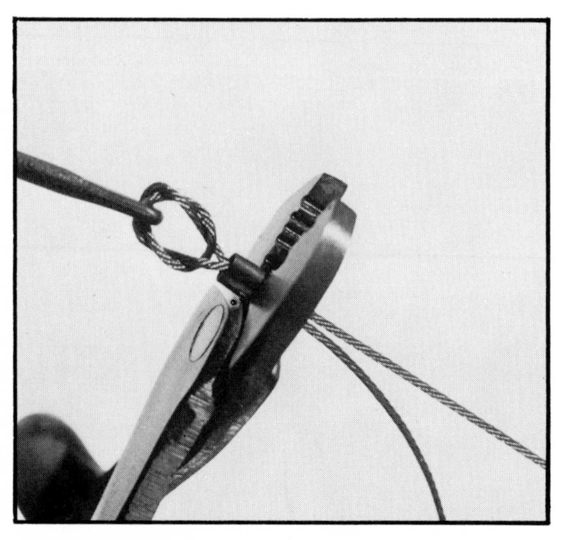

9. Use the special crimping pliers to crush the sleeve against the cable. Be sure the sleeve rests in the proper slot in the pliers.

10. Slide the second sleeve over the tag end. In this illustration, we have purposely exaggerated the distance between sleeves so that it would be clearer. In actual practice, the sleeves should be within one inch of each other. Otherwise, the loop between the tag end and standing part could trap air bubbles while trolling or the hook could fall back and through this loop.

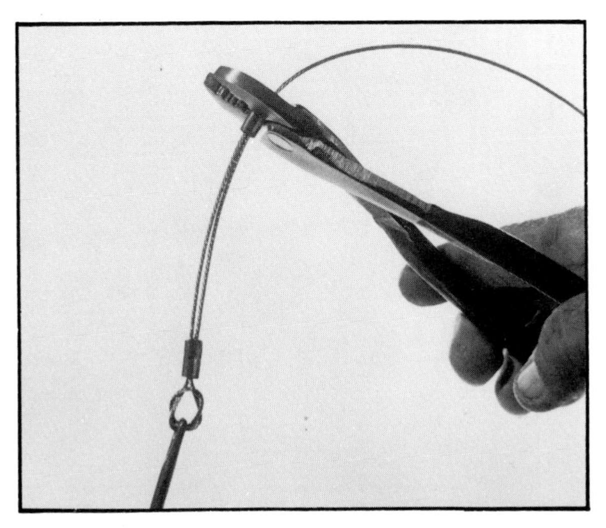

11. When the second sleeve is in position, crimp it securely with the special pliers. Make sure there is a one-inch distance between sleeves.

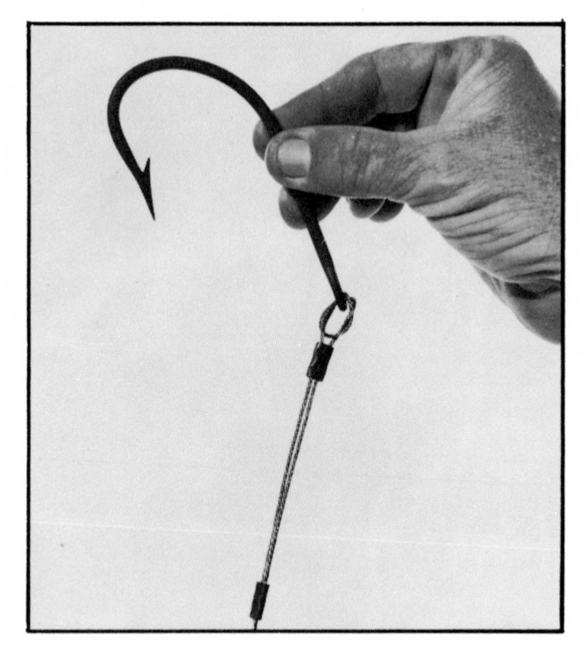

12. The completed connection looks like this.

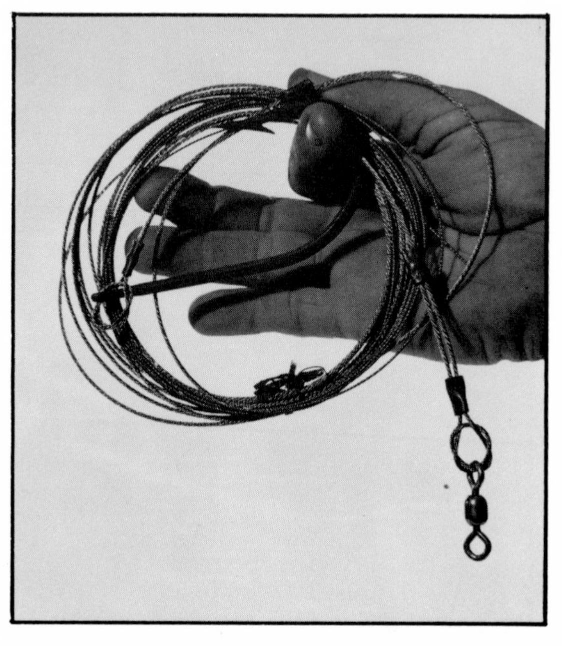

13. The same crimped loop is used to attach the swivel to the other end of the leader. Remember that these big-game leaders should be made up in advance and then stored for use.

QUICK-CHANGE WIRE WRAP

If you must use wire for protection against sharp teeth and don't need the strength of a Haywire Twist, you might prefer the Quick-change Wire Wrap. This knot makes it easy to change lures without having to cut the wire and then tie a new twist.

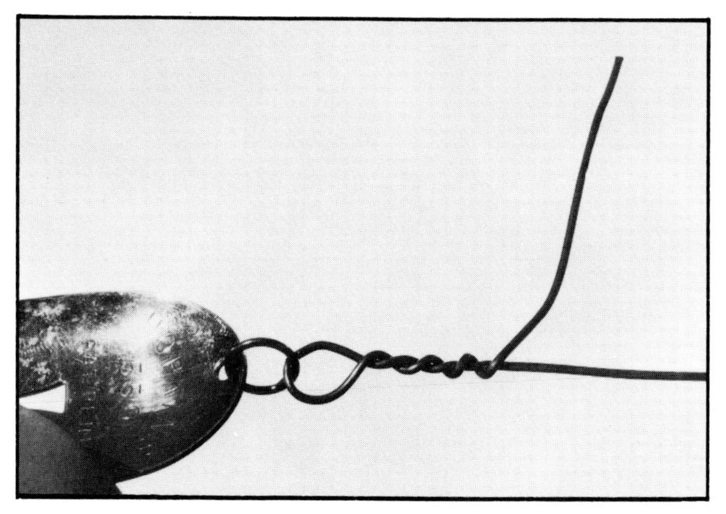

1. Insert the solid wire through the eye of a hook or lure. Make a round loop as you would to start a Haywire Twist. Then make several spiral wraps with the tag end around the standing part. Note that these are *not* barrel wraps (that is, close together and parallel).

2. Break the wire off as you would in the Haywire Twist and you have a finished knot.

3. When you want to change lures, simply unwrap the wire, insert the tag end through the eye of the new lure, and rewrap the wire along the same spirals.

TROLLING SPOON LOOP

There are times when it is necessary to use solid or plastic-coated wire for protection against fish with sharp teeth while trolling or casting a spoon. With solid wire, you could use a Haywire Twist if you made a large enough loop, or you could make a loop in plastic-coated wire. The problem is that a single strand of wire could kink or nick against the metal of the spoon. You can eliminate the risk and permit the spoon to swing through its maximum arc by using the Trolling Spoon Loop.

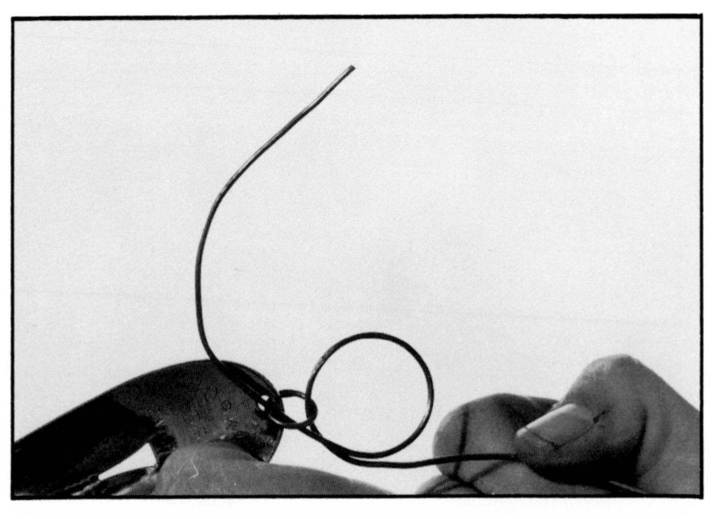

1. Pass the tag end of the wire through the eye of the spoon *twice,* forming a complete loop. Be sure to allow a tag end of at least twelve inches before beginning this knot.

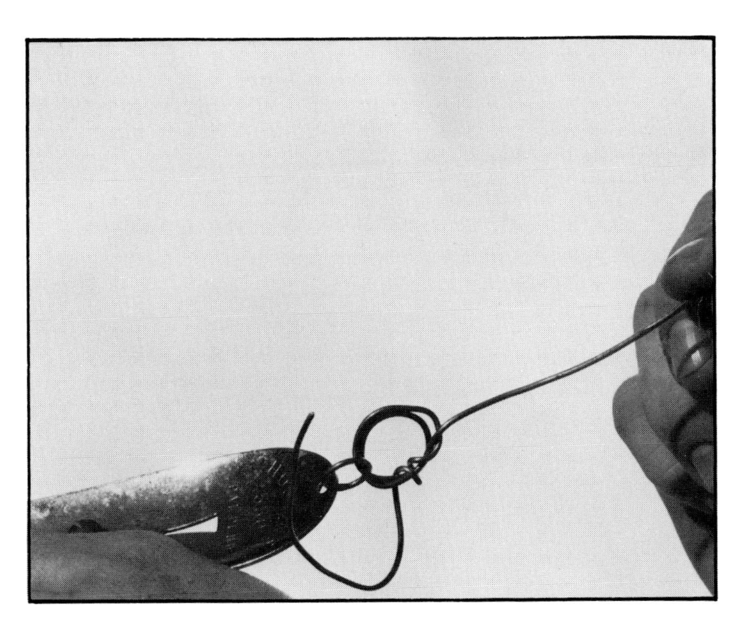

2. Bring the tag end past the standing part of the wire as if you were going to insert it through the eye of the spoon for a third time. However, after the tag end is past the standing part, wrap it in and out of the loops that have been formed. This is similar to the way you would tie the Jansik Special except that you continue wrapping all the way around the loops.

3. When the tag end has been wrapped around the loops to complete the circle, use a barrel wrap around the standing part to finish the knot. Break the wire if it is single strand as you would in the Haywire Twist. Plastic-coated wire can be twisted around the standing part and finished off with a Heated Twist.

Fly-fishing Knots

NAIL KNOT

Often called the Tube Knot because of the instrument used in tying, the Nail Knot makes an ideal connection between the butt section of the fly leader and the fly line. It is sometimes used in other tying situations such as attaching monofilament to Dacron. In that case, two Nail Knots would be tied back to back and then jammed together.

To tie the Nail Knot, you must have a hollow tube. There are a number of ways to obtain this tube ranging from hollow needles to the tips of fiberglass rod blanks. Some anglers are now using refill cartridges of ball-point pens after cutting the cartridge to the proper length and cleaning out the inside.

The Nail Knot is easier to tie than it looks and it is remarkably strong.

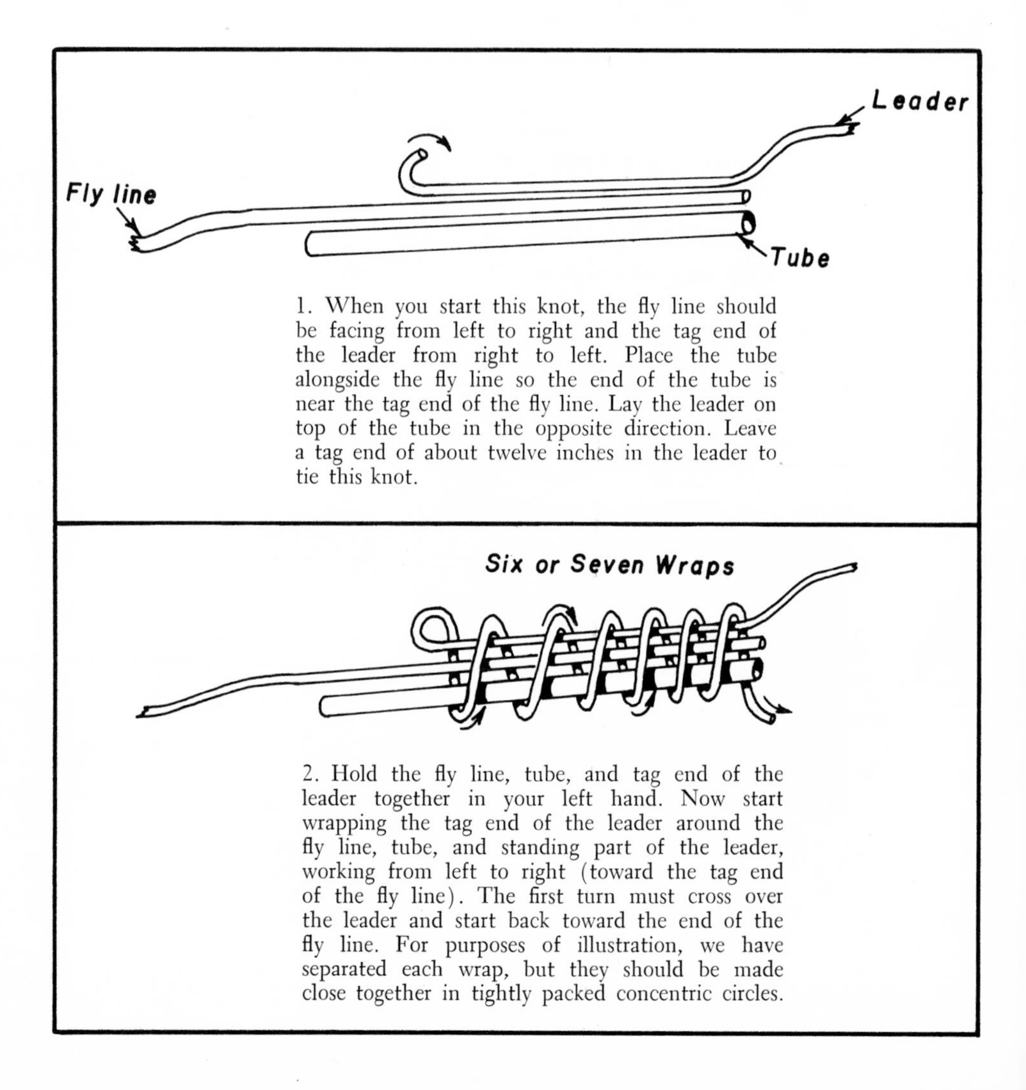

1. When you start this knot, the fly line should be facing from left to right and the tag end of the leader from right to left. Place the tube alongside the fly line so the end of the tube is near the tag end of the fly line. Lay the leader on top of the tube in the opposite direction. Leave a tag end of about twelve inches in the leader to tie this knot.

2. Hold the fly line, tube, and tag end of the leader together in your left hand. Now start wrapping the tag end of the leader around the fly line, tube, and standing part of the leader, working from left to right (toward the tag end of the fly line). The first turn must cross over the leader and start back toward the end of the fly line. For purposes of illustration, we have separated each wrap, but they should be made close together in tightly packed concentric circles.

3. When you have made six or seven wraps with the tag end of the leader, insert the tag end back through the center of the hollow tube. You're going to pull the tag end through the center of the wraps. When you first try this knot, you'll experience some difficulty in holding the turns tight with your left hand while you insert the tag end through the tube.

4. *You must hold the wraps securely while performing this step.* Slowly and carefully remove the tube. The tube is removed toward the standing part of the fly line and away from the standing part of the leader. Remember to keep holding the turns in place.

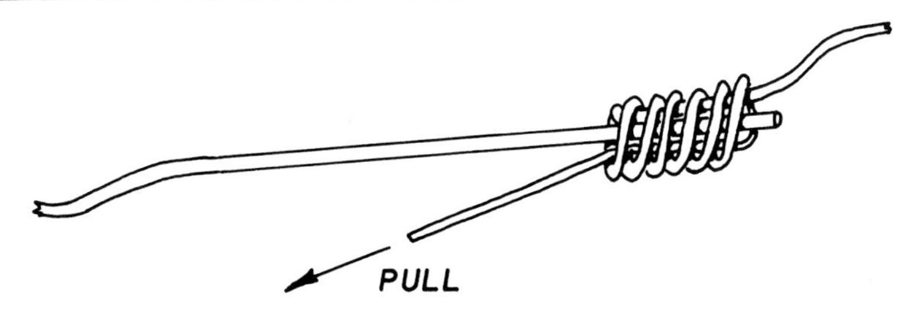

5. *Continue holding the turns.* Pull the tag end of the leader slowly and carefully to tighten the knot. When you feel the turns under your left hand begin to tighten, you can release your grip on the turns. How you tighten the knot after this stage is important. Moisten the knot first. Use pliers to grip the tag end of the leader. Pull the standing part at the same time with your other hand. After exerting uniform pull on both the tag end and standing part of the leader, pull the standing part of both the leader and fly line to make certain the Nail Knot won't slip.

6. Trim the tag end of the fly line and tag end of the leader. Then coat the Nail Knot with Pliobond cement or any other rubber-based cement. If you find that the turns of the knot tend to squeeze the fly line and not lie evenly (or if the knot is canted) you can circumvent this problem with another procedure in Step 5. As you tighten the Nail Knot by pulling on the tag end and standing part of the leader, hold the tag end of the fly line in your teeth and exert light pressure. This will cause the fly line to lie flat as the knot is tightened.

SPEED NAIL KNOT

Many fishermen find the Nail Knot difficult to tie and wouldn't want to be forced to fashion one at streamside or under less than ideal conditions. The Speed Nail Knot is the answer and it is one of our favorites. With a small sewing needle, you can tie a perfect Nail Knot every time and do it in less than a minute. Before you start on this one, review the section under Snelling a Hook. The Nail Knot is really nothing more than a snell. Here's how it is done.

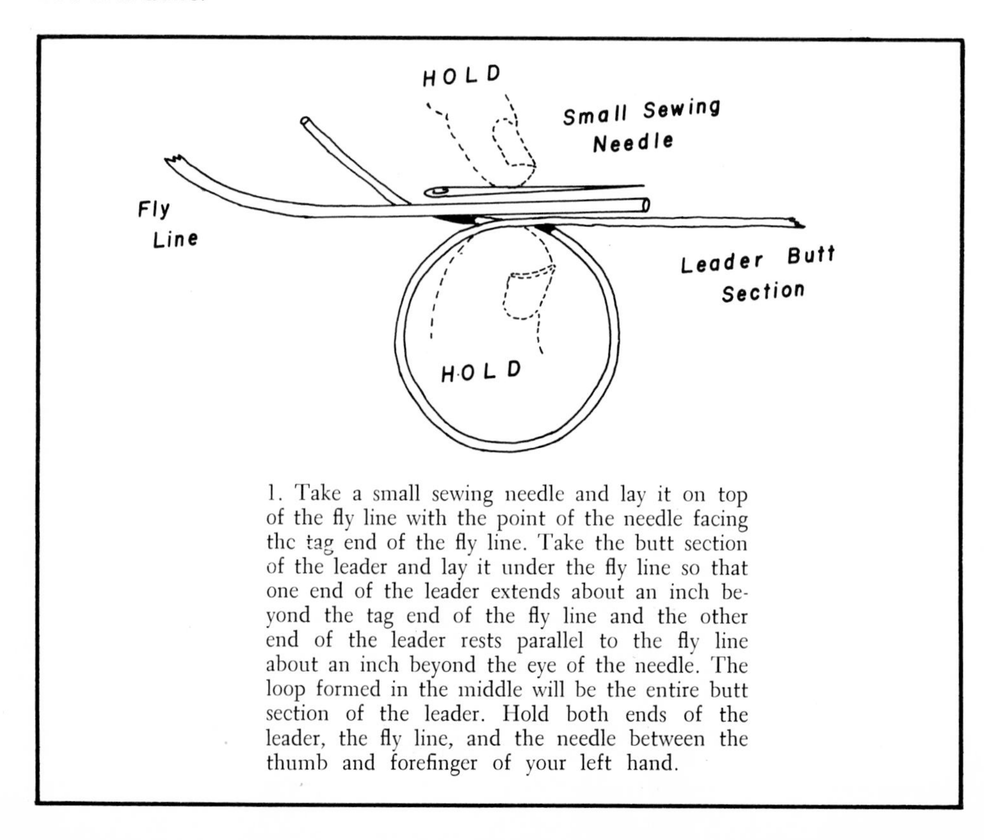

1. Take a small sewing needle and lay it on top of the fly line with the point of the needle facing the tag end of the fly line. Take the butt section of the leader and lay it under the fly line so that one end of the leader extends about an inch beyond the tag end of the fly line and the other end of the leader rests parallel to the fly line about an inch beyond the eye of the needle. The loop formed in the middle will be the entire butt section of the leader. Hold both ends of the leader, the fly line, and the needle between the thumb and forefinger of your left hand.

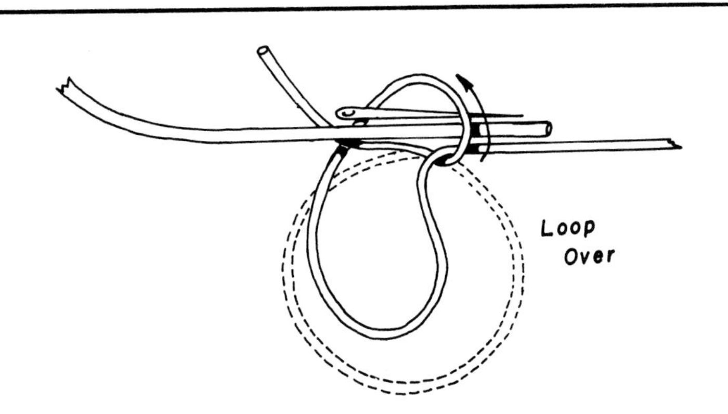

2. Take the leg of the leader loop closer to the tag end of the fly line in your right hand. Wrap it over the needle, fly line, and leader, working away from you.

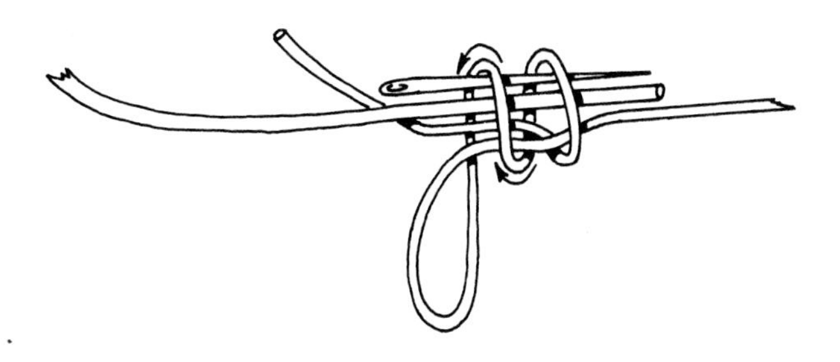

3. Continue wrapping the leader in a series of six or seven turns around the needle, fly line, and leader. Each wrap should lie alongside the preceding one. We have separated the wraps for purposes of illustration. Remember you are working toward the eye of the needle and away from the tag end of the fly line.

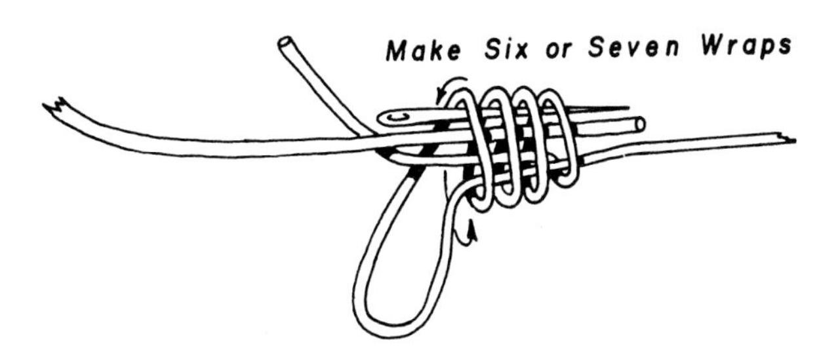

4. When you have made six or seven wraps, hold the wraps securely with the thumb and forefinger of your left hand. At the same time, pull the end of the leader that is extending beyond the tag end of the fly line. This will pull the big loop in the leader through the center of the wraps forming the Nail Knot.

PULL

PULL

PULL BOTH ENDS OF THE MONOFILAMENT UNTIL THE KNOT IS TIGHT

5. At this point, grip the tag end of the leader with pliers and the standing part of the leader in your right hand. Pull both ends slowly until the knot starts to tighten. Then, slide the needle out (pulling it out eye first toward the fly line). Finally, retighten the knot by pulling on both ends of the leader.

PULL

6. After the knot is tightened as outlined in Step 5, pull the standing part of the fly line and the standing part of the leader. The knot should be secure. Trim the tag ends of the leader and fly line and coat the knot with Pliobond cement or a similar rubber-based cement.

NEEDLE NAIL KNOT

This is unquestionably the best way to attach the butt section of the leader to a fly line, because the leader flows from the center of the fly line instead of coming off the side as it would in a regular Nail Knot. It will take a little patience to tie this knot the first time, but you'll soon get the idea.

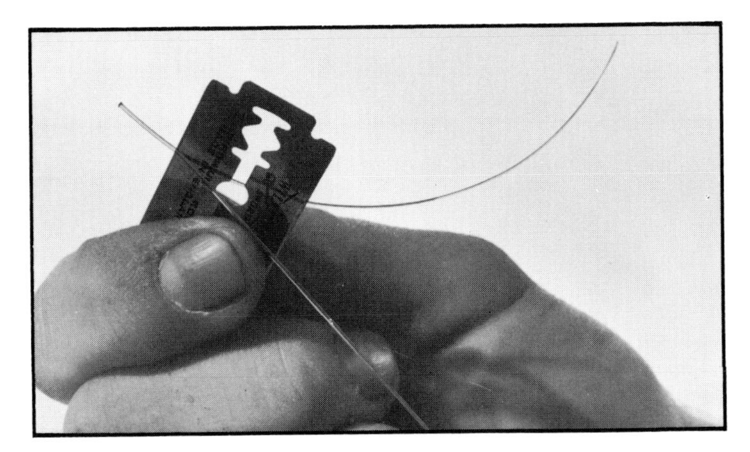

1. You will need a *brand-new* razor blade. Hold the tag end of the leader in your left hand about three inches from the bitter end with the curl in the monofilament facing *toward* you. The razor is in your right hand. Place the razor at about a 45° angle to the monofilament so that it bites into the mono (a little practice will help you find the correct angle). Make a smooth forward stroke with the razor and you will actually slice the monofilament. Several more strokes with the razor will produce a line that tapers to a hairlike point.

2. Insert the hairlike end of the monofilament into the eye of the *smallest* needle you have that will accept the monofilament. You must have a small diameter needle to do the job, so you might have to work at threading the mono through the eye.

3. Using pliers to hold the needle if necessary, insert the needle through the end of the fly line as shown.

4. Hold the fly line where it has been penetrated by the needle between the thumb and forefinger of your left hand. Grip the needle point with a pair of pliers and pull smoothly.

5. When the needle is pulled through the fly line, it will carry the monofilament butt section of the leader with it. Pull enough monofilament through the fly line to tie a Nail Knot.

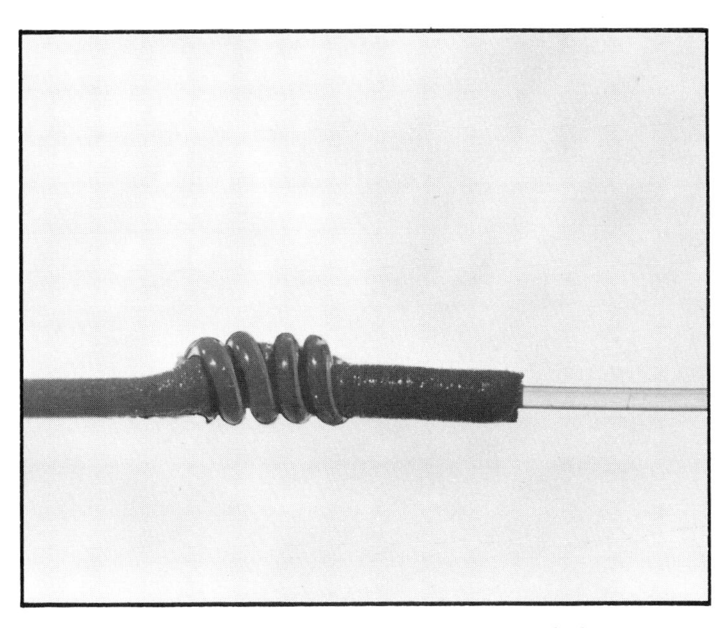

6. After you have tied a Nail Knot around the fly line (see separate instructions on Nail Knot), the finished Needle Nail Knot should look like this.

PUTTING A LOOP IN FLY LINE

Tackle dealers are often called upon to put a loop in fly line or connect the backing, because the angler in question lacks the confidence to make his own connections. Yet there is no guarantee that someone else will make the loop any better than you can do it. Making a loop in fly line is simple if you take your time. Here's how it is done.

1. A standard fly line is built over a center or core of braided line. The first task is to strip the coating off the fly line at the tag end of the running line (the part that goes on the reel first). Remember that you cannot do this with monofilament fly lines (*See* Special Instructions). You'll need a foot or two of *braided line* not exceeding twenty-pound test (monofilament won't work and neither will heavier braided lines). In this illustration, we have used a pencil to represent the fly line so you can see how a girth hitch is formed. Make a girth hitch around the fly line with the braided line about three inches in from the end. Draw the girth hitch tight by pulling on both ends together and working the hitch together with your fingernails. Once it cuts through the coating of the fly line, jerk the braided line quickly toward the tag end of the fly line. This should strip the coating off the fly line.

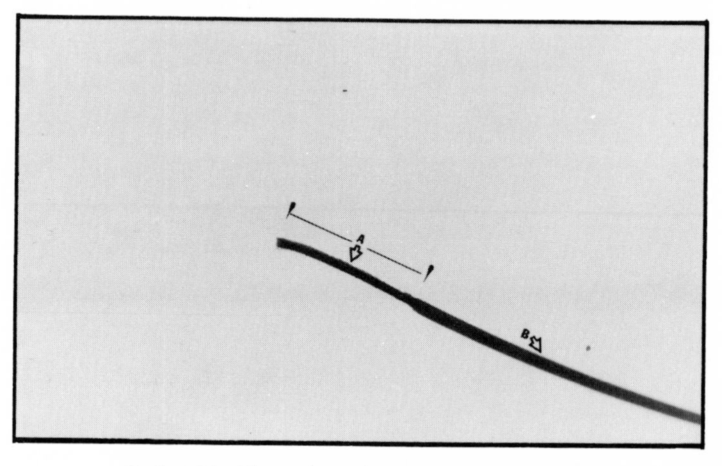

2. In this illustration, A represents the braided core of the fly line and B is the fly line with the coating. When you have completed Step 1, the fly line should look like this.

3. Double the fly line back to form a loop with the stripped portion of the tag end parallel to the standing part of the fly line.

4. You'll need a fly-tying bobbin with a spool of A thread for this step. Lay the tag end of the thread along the ends of the loop and make several turns with the bobbin until the thread is locked securely on the loop. Trim the excess thread that extends beyond these locking turns.

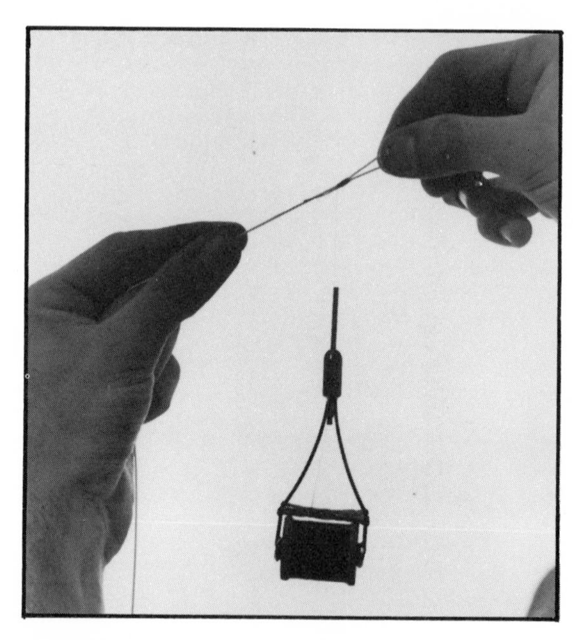

5. With a little practice, this step can be done easily. Attach a rubber band across the arms of the bobbin and just above the spool of thread to increase tension on the bobbin. Then hold the loop in one hand and the standing part of the fly line in the other. Swing the bobbin in a series of complete circles around the fly line, "walking" the bobbin down and back to lash the tag end of the fly line securely against the standing part. It's important to swing the bobbin under tension because this forces the thread to bind tightly. If you were to wrap it by hand, the thread would not be as tight.

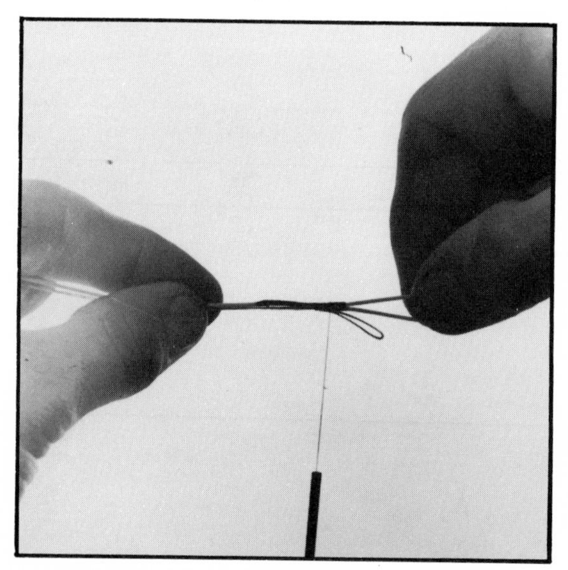

6. If you've ever wrapped a rod, you know how to finish off the windings. Take a short length of light monofilament or braided line and bend it in half forming a U. Lay the closed end of the U toward the loop in the fly line and wind another fifteen turns with the thread over the fly line and the U together. The turns should be made *toward the loop* in the fly line.

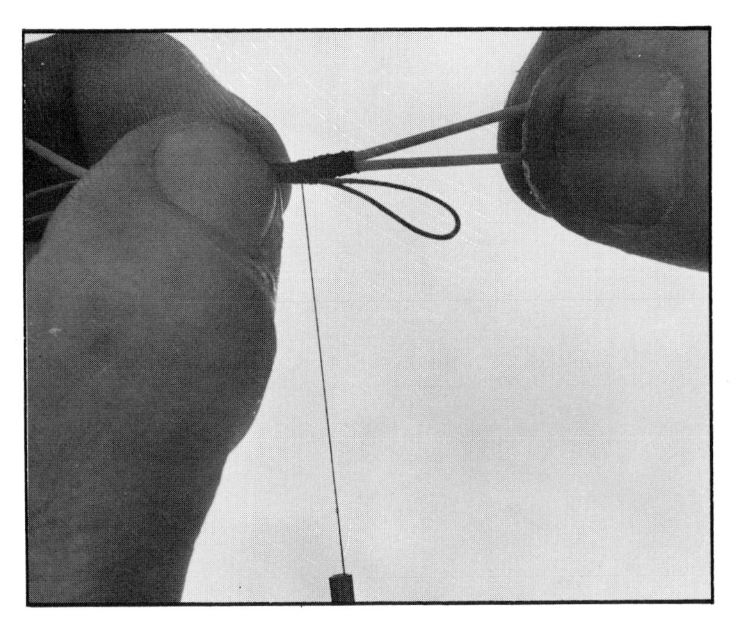

7. This close-up will show you what the wraps look like when you have taken fifteen turns around the fly line and the light mono or Dacron.

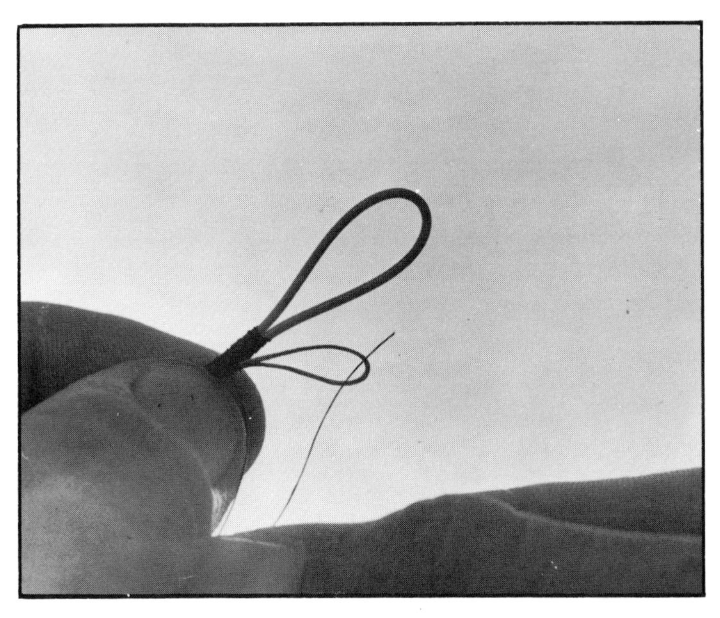

8. Cut the thread coming out of the bobbin and insert the tag end of the thread through the U in the light line.

9. Hold the fly line loop in one hand and the ends of the light line in the other. Pull the light line out from under the wraps, drawing the tag end of the thread that you just cut at the bobbin through the center of the wraps.

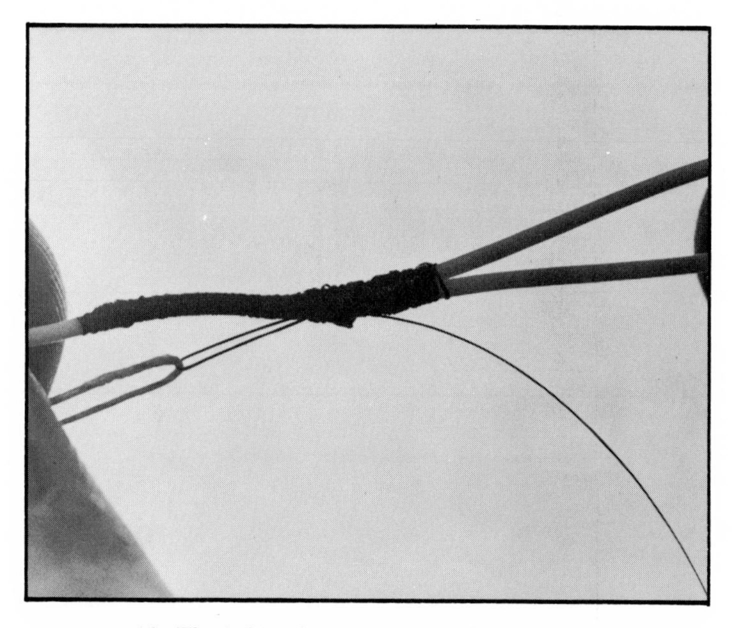

10. The lashing becomes secure when the thread passes inside the fifteen turns. Tighten the thread and trim it close to the point where it exits from under the turns.

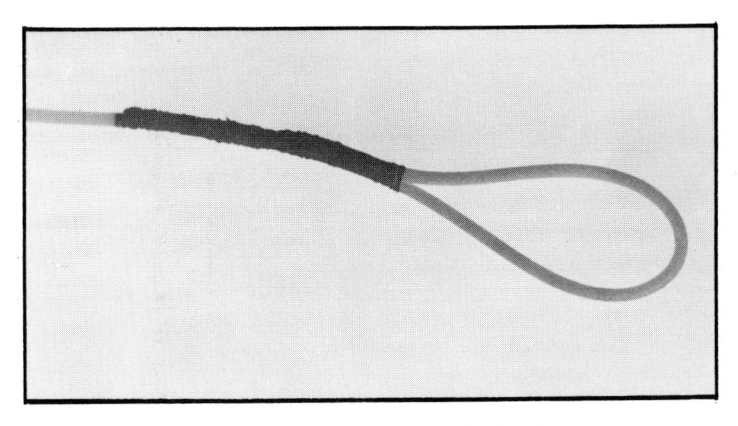

11. Put two or three coats of Pliobond cement or another rubber-based cement over the wrappings, letting the cement dry between coats. The finished loop will be amazingly strong.

PUTTING A LOOP IN MONOFILAMENT FLY LINE

The best way to attach Dacron backing to any fly line is with interlocking loops. This permits you to switch fly lines rapidly and it also makes an exceedingly strong connection that flows through the rod guides easily. Unlike the standard fly lines that are built on a core of braided line, monofilament fly lines are extruded and lack the braided line in the center. Because of this, you cannot use standard knots and expect them to hold. It should be mentioned that monofilament fly lines lack the strength of standard fly lines. Manufacturers are still working on this problem and some of the mono fly lines have been improved, but if you're after big fish, you should be aware of this shortcoming.

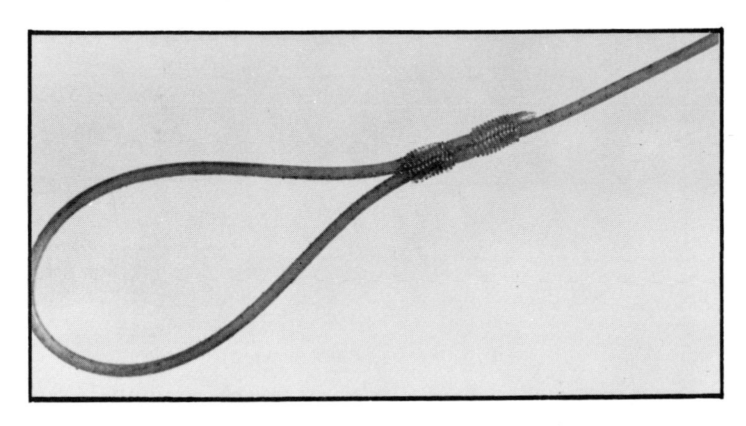

1. To make a loop in the end of monofilament fly line, cut the tag end of the fly line at a 45° angle. Then, tie two Speed Nail Knots about ¼ to ⅜ inches apart. Coat the finished knots with Pliobond or any other rubber-based cement. The finished loop will look like this illustration and it will form a neat connection.

INTERLOCKING LOOPS

In several sections of this book, we refer to interlocking loops as a means of connecting two lines. It is imperative that the loops be interlocked correctly or you will lose substantial strength.

1. If a girth hitch is used as the interlocking connection, you will sacrifice considerable strength and there is every possibility that one line will cut through the other. Instead, the loops should interlock in the form of a Square Knot, correctly distributing the stress.

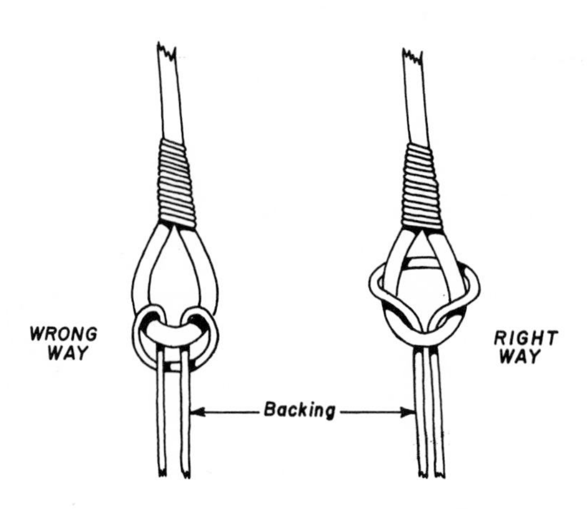

2. This is the way an interlocking loop should look when it is tightened.

PUTTING A LOOP IN DACRON

A braided line such as Dacron can be spliced quickly to form a loop, eliminating the need for knots and providing an extremely strong connection. Fly-fishermen prefer this splice to knots because it will run through the guides freely if a fish takes out all the fly line and gets down to the backing. The loop created can be interlocked with a loop at the end of the fly line. Splices in Dacron can also be used for a number of other assignments where a loop is needed. Following a similar splicing principle, you can also connect two lengths of Dacron in basically the same manner.

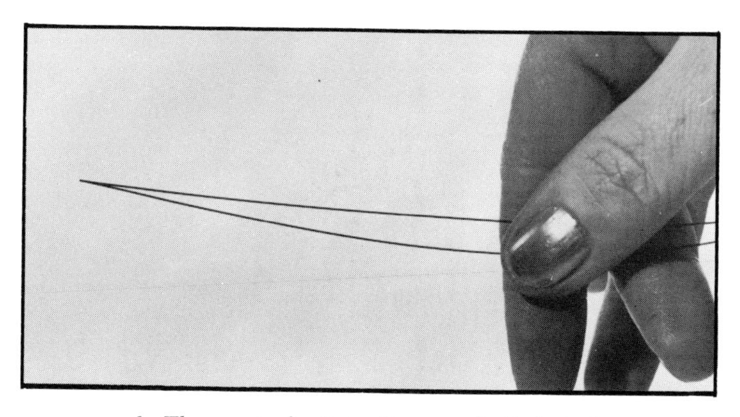

1. The secret of splicing Dacron effectively is the tool that you use. Most line manufacturers supply a sophisticated splicing tool that can cause more trouble than it is worth. Your best bet is to make your own tool by making a sharp modified V bend in a very thin piece of wire (#3 trolling wire is an ideal choice). The bend in the wire should be severe so that a point is formed.

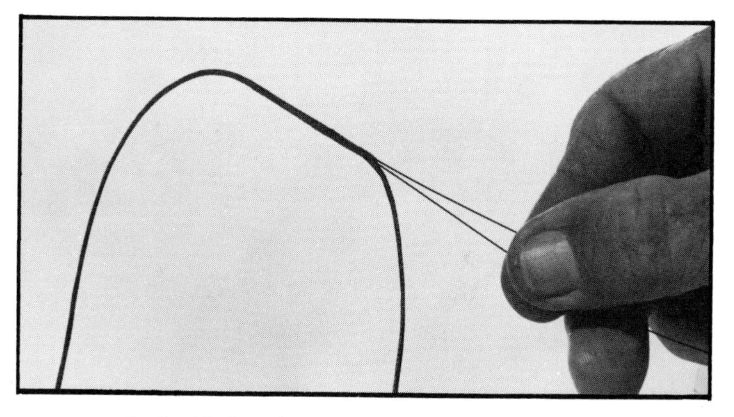

2. Decide how big a loop you want to make and how long a splice you will need. A six- or eight-inch splice is as strong as you will ever need. Hold the Dacron in your left hand and insert the point of your splicing tool into the center of the Dacron. It might take a minute or so to work the point into the hollow center, but with practice, you can do it quickly.

3. You'll discover that the braid in Dacron is similar to the weave in the old Chinese finger trick you might have played with as a youngster. That's the one where you push one finger in either end, but you can't pull your fingers apart because the weave tightens. Use your left hand to push the Dacron back on your splicing needle and keep working the needle through the core of the line until you have a long enough area for the splice. Then push the splicing needle back through the outside of the line.

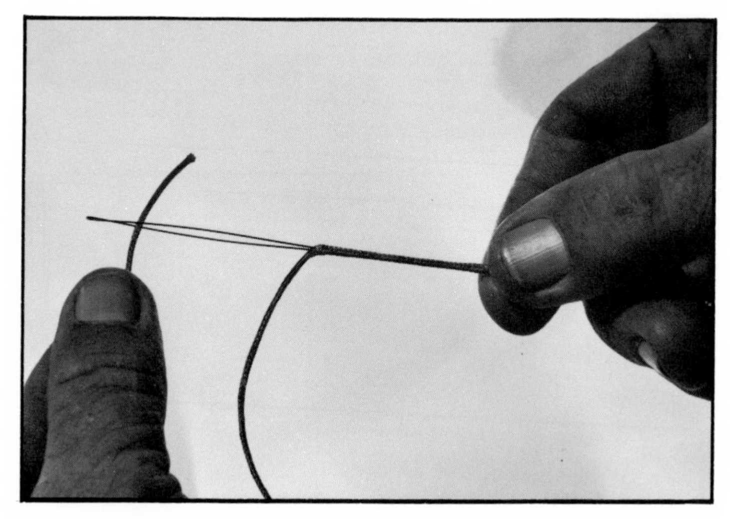

4. Insert the tag end of the Dacron through the wire loop, leaving about an inch or two extending through the loop. With your left hand, push up on the Dacron that is over the wire. By pushing forward, the Dacron weave will open slightly and enable you to pull the wire back through the center of the Dacron. As you pull the wire out, the tag end will follow and the splice will be made.

5. Note in this photograph how the Dacron in front of the fingers is being compressed. This allows the tag end to pass through the middle. When the tag end has been pulled completely through the center of the standing part, trim the excess.

6. To tighten the splice, pull on the loop with one hand while holding the standing part with the other. Sometimes anglers want to insure that there is even more strength in the splice. They do this by putting a second splice in the Dacron. When they pull the tag end through the first splice, they allow an extra length. Instead of trimming the knot, they insert the splicing needle back in the standing part and work toward the first splice. Two or three inches of the tag end remain outside and parallel to the standing part. Then the tag end is buried in the second splice.

BLOOD KNOT DROPPER LOOP

Although the use of a dropper fly is primarily a technique employed by fly-fishermen, it has also found favor among casting enthusiasts who are now rigging a streamer fly or small lure in front of a big plug or bucktail. In fly-fishing, this approach performs well with nymphs, wet flies, and even streamers or bucktails. However, it is seldom used with dry flies or popping bugs.

A number of fishermen still insist on tying a dropper loop in the leader, but research has shown that many of these loops are not strong and reduce the breaking strength of the leader. A better way to achieve the same results is through the use of a Blood Knot to attach the final tippet section.

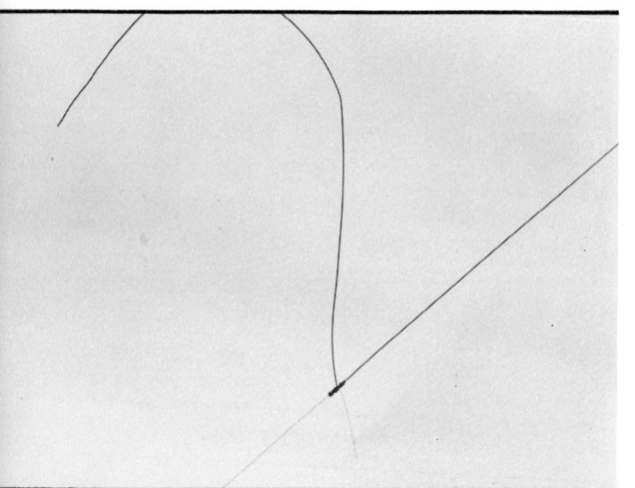

1. In the illustration, the darker line represents the heavier section of leader material. The Blood Knot is tied in the normal manner with the exception that the tag end of the heavier leader is permitted to extend eight to ten inches beyond the finished knot. The tag end of the lighter line is trimmed close to the knot.

2. The dropper fly is tied directly to the tag end of the heavier leader section. Because the leader is heavier, it is stiffer and will tend to hold the fly away from the rest of the leader. With this system, two or three flies can be fished simultaneously without sacrificing knot strength.

Boating Knots

BOWLINE

The Bowline ranks as one of the most useful knots you can learn. It forms a loop that will not slip or jam, can be tied easily and quickly, and that you can untie in an instant regardless of how tight it is.

1. The palms of your hands should be open and facing up toward you (fingers would be pointing directly away from you). There should be a comfortable distance between the two hands. Lay the line across your hands so that the tag end extends slightly beyond your right palm and the standing part cuts across your left palm. Let a belly in the line hang loosely between your two hands. Holding the line as outlined, extend your right hand and arm (with the tag end of the line) around the post. At the same time, meet your right hand with the left hand and the standing part of the line. Tie a simple overhand knot. Transfer the tag end to your left hand and slide both standing part and tag end around the post so that the knot is now in front of you.

2. You will need about one foot of tag end to complete the knot, so make any necessary adjustments. By pulling on the tag end, you will form a half hitch. Look at the knot closely at this stage. As you face the post, the tag end will be coming around the left side and passing through a loop that was formed in the standing part.

3. Hold the loop formed in the standing part in your left hand as shown. Take the tag end of the line in your right hand. Pass the tag end *under* the standing part and insert it back in the loop that you are holding with your left hand. The tag end goes *inside* of the standing part.

4. Look closely at this illustration to make sure you have formed the knot properly. The tag end passes *under* the standing part and goes back in the loop on the *inside*.

5. To tighten the knot, alternately pull on the tag end and the standing part. You'll have to work the knot to tighten it properly. You can open a Bowline quickly by pushing the standing part toward the knot while you push one side of the loop toward the standing part with the other hand.

SQUARE KNOT

The Square Knot ranks near the top of the most familiar knots. It is a quick and excellent way to join two lines of relatively the same diameter. You can also use the Square Knot for lines of unequal diameter, but you should secure both tag ends to the standing parts so that it cannot slip. This knot works best when there is tension on both lines.

1. Hold the tag end of one line in your right hand and the tag end of the second line in your left hand. You'll need about six inches of each tag end to tie the knot. Lay the tag end in your left hand on top of and across the tag end in your right hand. This will form an X with the points of the tag ends facing away from you. Then bring the tag end in your left hand under the tag end in your right hand, forming a simple overhand knot.

2. Now reverse the procedure. Lay the tag end in your right hand across the tag end in your left hand and make another overhand knot.

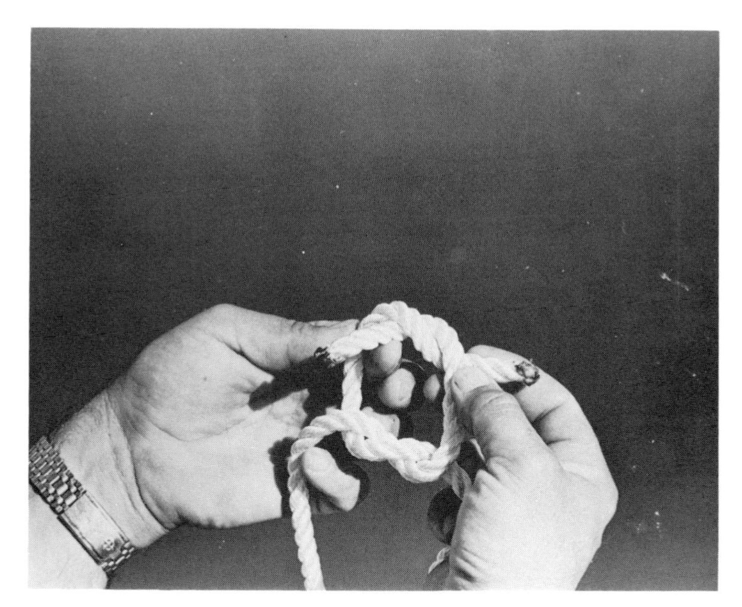

3. When you finish the second overhand knot, hold the tag end on each side against the standing part on that side and pull all four strands apart at the same time. This will tighten the knot. To loosen the knot, push the tag ends and standing parts toward each other.

4. On each side of the knot, both the tag end and the standing part must be parallel. Otherwise, you have tied a Granny Knot. A Square Knot is simple if you remember *right over left, left over right.*

TWO HALF HITCHES

Two half hitches make a speedy and easy way to tie a line from your boat to a ring, post, or other object. It is considered a temporary knot because it is not as secure as some of the others. Half hitches are also used to finish off knots for extra security.

1. Pass the tag end of the line around the post or through the ring to which it is to be tied. Make a simple overhand knot.

2. Pull the tag end toward you and parallel to the standing part. This will change the overhand knot into a Half Hitch.

3. Now make another overhand knot around the standing part of the line. Pull the tag end so that the overhand knot becomes a second Half Hitch.

4. Slide the two Half Hitches against each other and then push the knot against the object to which it is tied.

SHEET BEND

Most knot experts consider the Sheet Bend to be one of the ten indispensable knots you can learn to tie. You can connect two lines of very unequal diameter to one another with this knot in a matter of seconds and it is relatively strong.

1. Start by bringing the tag end of the larger line back and alongside the standing part to form a loop. Hold this loop in your left hand.

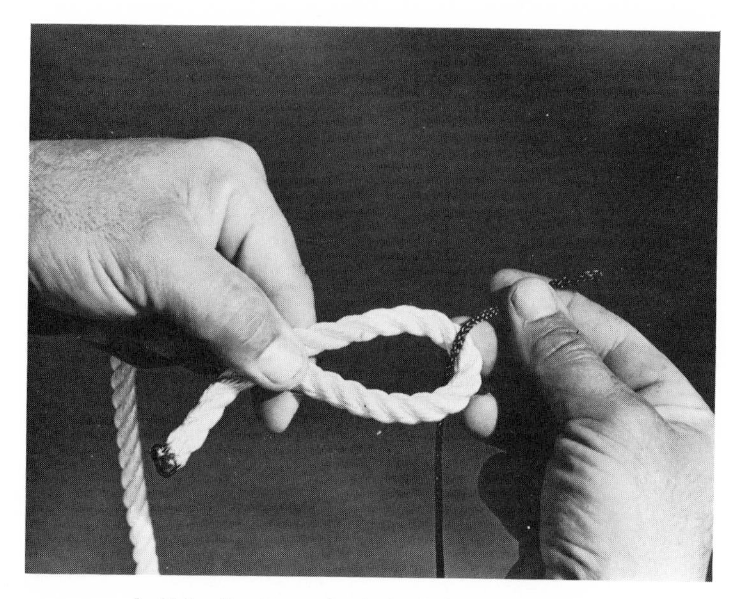

2. Take the tag end of the lighter line in your right hand. Bring it through the loop in the larger line *from the bottom to the top* as illustrated.

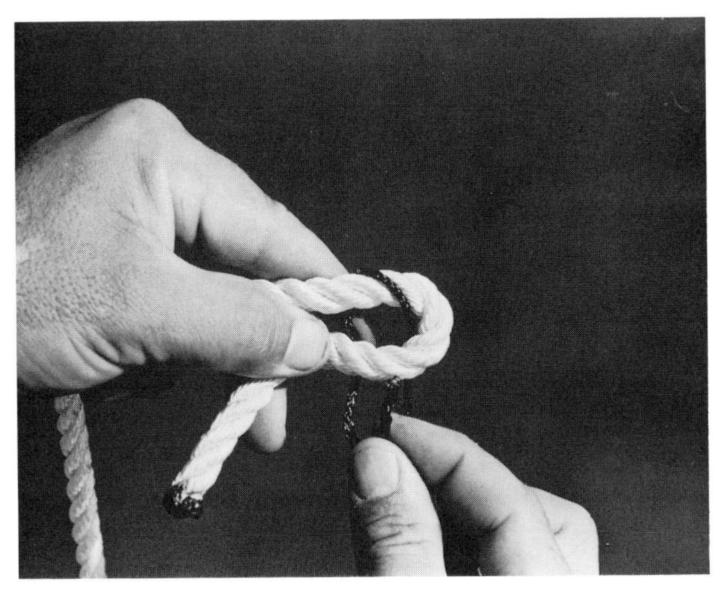

3. Pass the tag end of the lighter line completely around both sides of the loop in the larger line.

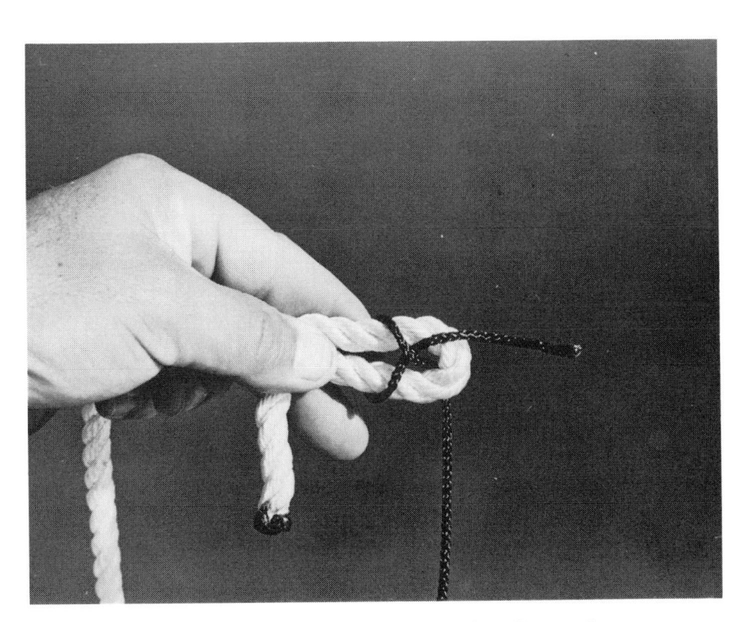

4. Then pass the tag end of the lighter line under the standing part of the lighter line so that the tag end of the lighter line is locked and rests securely on top of the loop. For an even stronger knot, you can make a Double Sheet Bend by passing the tag end of the light line around the two strands of the loop a second time and passing it under the standing part of the light line again.

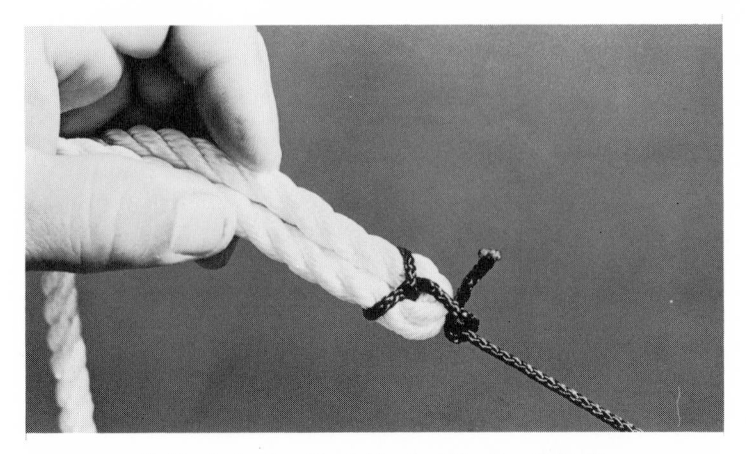

5. To lock the Sheet Bend, slide the light line toward the end of the loop in the larger line. Pull the standing part of the light line while holding both strands of the loop in the larger line. If you use a single Sheet Bend, tie a Half Hitch or two with the tag end of the light line around the standing part of the light line for extra security.

CLOVE HITCH

The Clove Hitch is a favorite knot among small boatmen for tying to a dock quickly. It is also used by shallow water fishermen for tying a light bow line to a pushpole that has been thrust into the bottom of the flats. Although it can be tied rapidly, the Clove Hitch is not always easy to untie. Pressure causes it to bind tightly and, when it is wet, it's nearly impossible to work the strands loose.

1. Take the tag end of the line in your right hand, while holding the standing part in your left hand. Pass the tag end around the post and *under* the standing part.

2. Repeat the procedure a second time (pass the tag end around the post and *under the standing part*) and you have tied a Clove Hitch. If the top of the post is accessible, you can form a loop by passing the tag end *under* the standing part and slide the loop on the pole.

3. To tighten the knot, pull the tag end in one direction and the standing part in the other. You can also slide the two loops around the pole close together to keep the knot from slipping. Then, if you want to make the tie even more secure, use the tag end to put a Half Hitch or two around the standing part.

STORING SURPLUS LINE ON A CLEAT

The competence of any boat handler or crew member is often judged by his attention to details. This is particularly true in the narrow confines of a marina or docking area. Loose line can be a problem and a dangerous one. Lines dumped unceremoniously in the cockpit of a boat or tossed freely across a dock are the mark of a novice. Surplus line can be stored neatly on a cleat if you will follow this procedure.

1. Slip the loop on the end of the line through the center of the cleat and bring it over both ends. Then coil all the loose line in concentric circles.

2. Leave a few feet of loose line between the coils and the cleat. Hold the coils in your left hand. Push the loose line between the coils and the cleat through the center of the coils and hold it in your right hand. Now make several twists in this short length of line with your right hand.

3. Hang the loop of twisted line back over the cleat and it will hold the coils neatly and securely. Remove the loop from the cleat and the line is coiled and ready for use.

SPLICING DIAMOND BRAIDED ROPE

A number of small boats are now equipped with lines made from Diamond Braided Rope because it is economical, relatively strong for small boats, and impervious to the elements. Although it can be knotted, knots tend to be bulky and the best method of putting a loop in the end is with a splice.

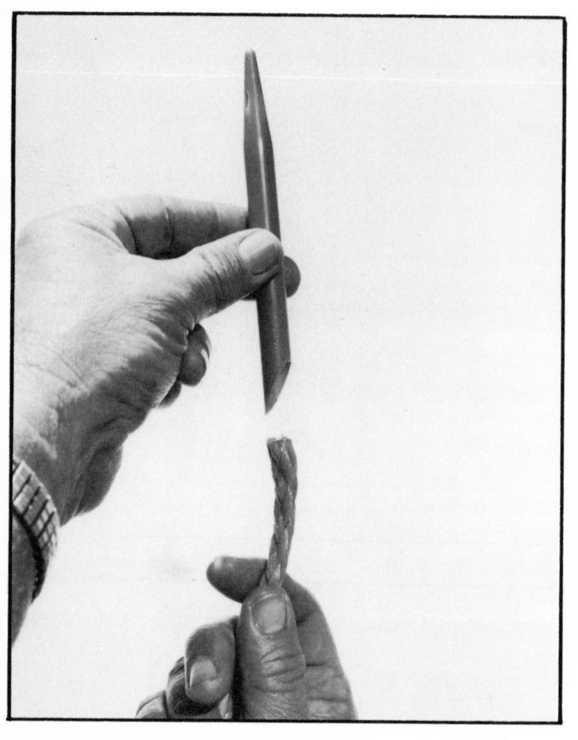

1. The easiest way of splicing Diamond Braided Rope is with a modified fid or splicing tool. Most of these tools are made from plastic and can be purchased at nominal cost where you buy the rope. You must have the right size tool for the rope you are using. In this example, we are using a ⅜-inch tool for ⅜-inch rope.

2. Insert the rope in the back of the splicing tool as far as it will go. Determine how big a loop you want and push the tool with the tag end of the line through the standing part at the spot where you want the loop to rejoin the standing part of the line.

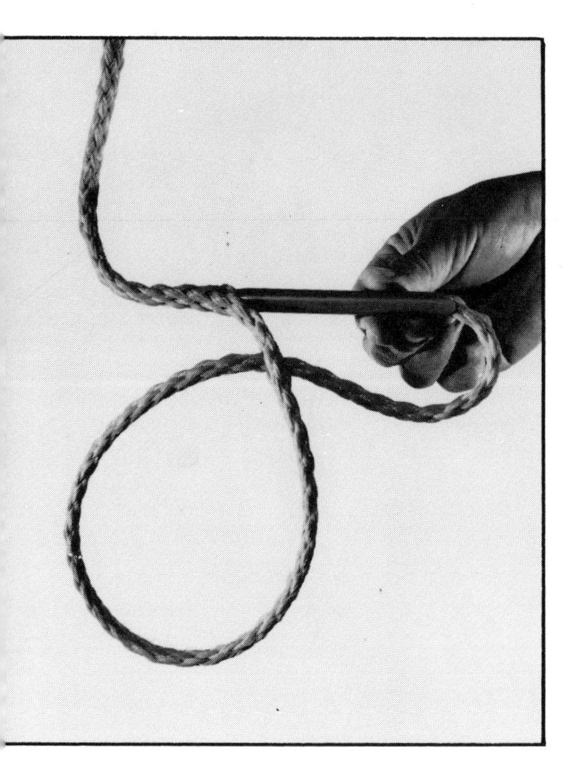

3. Leave yourself enough tag end to complete the splice. After drawing the tool and tag end completely through the standing part at the point you want the loop to form, push the tool through the center of the line as illustrated. Be sure to leave an inch or two of standing part between the spot where you formed the loop and the place where you insert the tool.

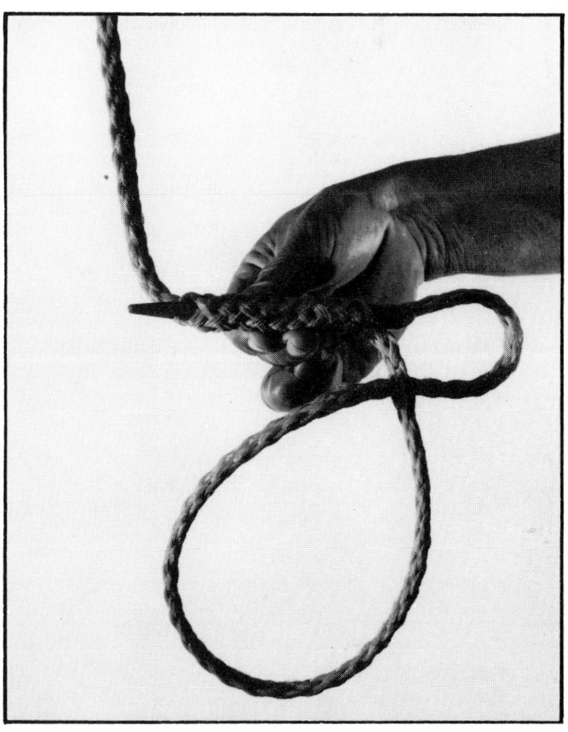

4. Run the splicing needle and tag end through the center of the standing part for the length of the tool. Then, pull the tool and tag end through the hollow center.

5. Leave another space of an inch or two and reinsert the tool and tag end through the hollow center of the rope a second time.

6. The tag end of the rope remains buried inside the core near the tail of the second splice. Withdraw the splicing tool.

7. The finished splice is smooth and strong. To make sure it is tight, pull on the loop and standing part of the rope at the same time.

5 PUTTING KNOTS TO WORK

KNOTS IN COMBINATION

It's one thing to tie a hook to the end of the line, put a loop in a leader, or twist some wire, and it's quite another when you must employ a series of knots to rig tackle. Knots in combination are more of a mental attitude plaguing anglers than a physical tying problem. The key is to look at each knot as an individual effort. After all, if you tie one weak knot, you've destroyed the system.

Selecting the right knots for the assignment is not difficult. In fact, the best procedure is to concentrate on a system that encompasses knots you can tie effectively and consistently. As you improve your knot-tying ability on individual knots, you can improve your knot system. Of course, the knots of greatest concern are those tied in the weakest section of line. If you can use a Bimini Twist in the weak portion, you can eliminate the problem. The only exceptions would be in delicate freshwater leaders and where a leader is not needed.

The most important aspect of rigging lines and leaders is thinking through the problem. Ask yourself what you are trying to accomplish and then pick the knots best suited to the task. There are many ways of rigging tackle, but only a handful of methods currently in use will stand the test of maximum pressure. Applying maximum pressure is the most significant factor in landing big fish: if the knots fail before that point, you're beaten before you ever set the hook.

Here are some of the ways in which we rig our terminal tackle. Our own fishing assignments take us all over the world in both fresh water and salt, where we are challenged by a wide range of fishing conditions and species. Yet the same methods seem to work in all these places and they should perform for you wherever you choose to fish.

FRESHWATER FLY LEADERS

The majority of freshwater fly-fishermen buy ready-made leaders either because they feel it is too complicated to make their own or they have doubts about their ability to tie knots. The beauty of making your own, however, is that you can achieve any taper you want.

In most tackle shops, you can purchase knotless or knotted tapered leaders depending on your personal preference. If you do buy your leaders, you should be aware that many of them have one shortcoming. The butt section of the leader is seldom heavy enough for easy casting and the leader tends to collapse on the cast at the point where it is joined to the fly line. The butt section of a leader should be about two-thirds the diameter of the tippet end of the fly line.

You can correct this by adding your own heavier butt section to the ready-made leader. Connect the butt section to the fly line with a Nail Knot or a Needle Knot. Then, tie a Double Surgeon's Loop in the end of your butt section and use the system of loops (illustrated later in this chapter) to make the connection. Or, simply tie a Blood Knot to join the two sections. With the heavier butt section, you'll find that your leaders will cast better.

Let's assume, however, that you do want to make your own leaders or at least know how it is done. There are a multitude of formulae kicking around. Many of these procedures are valid, but the problem is that most are just too complicated for average use. Recognize, also, that you are going to be fishing for different species and in different types of water. All of this will have a bearing on the length and taper of the leader you use. If you are fishing for northern pike, for example, you may want to use the basic saltwater taper or a modified freshwater version. Trout fishing in clear, shallow water requires a long, fine leader; fishing for trout in heavy water permits more latitude with leaders.

If you are trying to get a fly deep in fast-moving water, a short leader will do a better job than a longer one because monofilament tends to buoy the fly. If you're tossing a bass bug along a shoreline, leader length is equally important; it's a tough job to cast a heavy bug or fly with a long leader.

You can be successful in practically any freshwater fishing situation with a single leader formula. We like to call it the 60–20–20 method. The numbers are nothing more than percentages of total leader length. If you can remember those three numbers, you can tie a leader. To understand this principle, consider that every leader has three sections—the heavy rear or butt section, the hinge or mid-area of the leader, and the light tippet section. Our 60–20–20 formula merely tells you what percentage of the leader should fall in each section. Your own experience will guide you in making a leader for specific conditions, but as long as you follow this formula, it doesn't matter whether the leader is heavy or light.

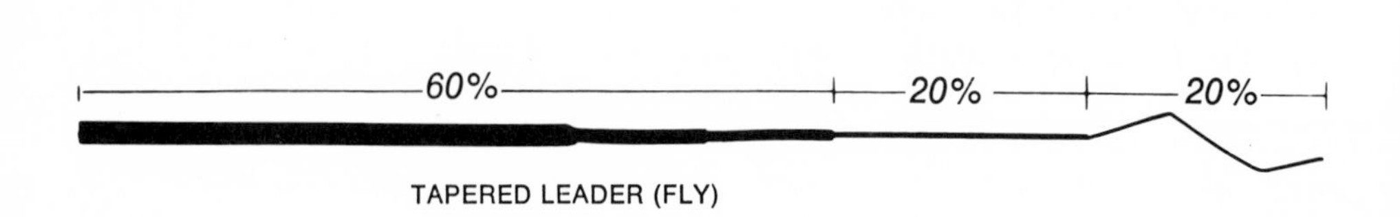

TAPERED LEADER (FLY)

Whenever you construct a freshwater leader, 60% of its length should be in the heavy butt section, 20% in the hinge, and 20% in the tippet. For simplicity of mathematics, let's use a ten-foot leader as an example. The butt section will be six feet long, the hinge or midsection will be two feet long, and you'll have a tippet that is two feet long. Conceivably, you could do this with three pieces of monofilament such as a twenty-five-pound-test butt section, a twelve-pound-test midsection, and a six-pound-test tippet. However, a leader should have a more progressive taper for better casting performance.

You can take the same formula and put a gradual taper in the leader. Let's rebuild our ten-foot leader for heavy trout fishing or bass fishing. We know that the total butt section must be six feet long. Instead of using six feet of twenty-five-pound test, use four feet of twenty-five-pound test. Then, tie in one foot of twenty-pound test and another foot of seventeen- or eighteen-pound test. We have now tapered the butt section from twenty-five-pound test to eighteen-pound test, but it is still six feet long.

In this example, the formula will allow us to use a hinge or mid-area that is two feet long. We can taper this by using six-inch pieces of fifteen-, twelve-, ten-, and eight-pound test. Or, we can shortcut this operation by eliminating one or two of these sizes. This will become a matter of experience and personal preference. Finally, our tippet section will be two feet long and comprised of a single test. In this case, we might choose six-pound test.

If you follow this basic 60–20–20 formula, you can vary it slightly to meet almost any challenge. In clear, shallow water, add a slightly longer tippet, and if you are using heavier flies or bugs, you won't need as much of a taper.

In constructing your own leader, each section is attached to the next one with a Blood Knot. The butt section of the leader is connected to the fly line with a Needle Knot or a Nail Knot. You also have the option of using the quick-change tippet, which we will discuss below.

THE LEVEL BASS BUG LEADER

A properly constructed tapered leader is always easier to turn over on a cast than a level leader. However, there are times when the best system must be pushed aside to gain practicality and catch fish. The Level Bass Bug Leader is a special application and it is valid only for bass where the vegetation in the water could cause problems. If you were to use a knotted leader, you would soon discover that you spent more time picking weeds and fine strands of grass from the knots than the time you spent fishing.

To circumvent this difficulty you can use a completely level leader made from a single strand of monofilament. The leader should be about six feet long (but it could range to eight feet) and you can use heavier material than you normally would because the weeds tend to break up the pattern of the leader on the water and the shadow of the leader on the bottom. Visibility to the fish is not a problem. Select a breaking strength heavy enough to carry the bass bug and attach it to the fly line with a Needle or Nail Knot. Then, simply tie the bass bug on the other end and start fishing.

If you want a lighter tippet, use a medium-length butt section of heavy monofilament and then tie in a lighter tippet. That way, you will only have one knot to contend with instead of the normal number in a standard taper.

In casting a level leader, you will also discover that you must build up line speed during the cast. That requires what we term "loop control" and you should be able to throw a tight loop that will force any leader to turn over properly. The fly line should be a weight forward (either of the saltwater variety or a standard bass bug taper) and if you know how to double haul on the cast, this will also help you to build up the line speed necessary to turn the leader over.

FRESHWATER QUICK-CHANGE TIPPET

The finer the leader material, the more difficult it is for an angler to change flies at streamside or tie on a new section of leader tippet. Hairlike diameters of monofilament force older anglers to resort to their bifocals or a magnifying glass. Even young fishermen have trouble holding delicate tippet material in their fingers while tying knots.

A series of experiments a few years back taught us that the weakest knot in any tapered leader is the one that connects the final tippet section to the rest of the leader. Even though it is the same Blood Knot that connects every other section of leader, that's the one that invariably breaks before any other part of the leader.

To solve the problem of strengthening this connection as well as eliminating the frustrations of tying tippets, we developed a system of interconnected loops that works well. At the point in your leader construction where

FLY LINE

LOOP-TO-LOOP

TIPPET

FRESH WATER LEADER
QUICK CHANGE TIPPET

you tie on the tippet, put a Double Surgeon's Loop in the main part of your leaders. Put another Double Surgeon's Loop in one end of the tippet section. By interconnecting these loops (slipping one through the other) you can change tippets in an instant.

The interlocked loops make a surprisingly strong connection and offer the advantage of enabling you to change tippet sections at streamside without a problem. The looped tippets can be made up in the comfort of your home when you don't have to fumble while facing rising fish. And if you want to go from a 3X to a 6X tippet, you can do so in a matter of seconds.

You might even want to carry the system one step further. If you know the waters you are fishing, you probably have a pretty good idea of the fly patterns that are most productive and the tippet strengths you will require. So you can make up complete tippet sections in advance with the basic flies tied to the end of the tippet. Then, when you want to change flies, there are no knots to tie. Instead, you merely change entire tippets with the flies already attached. Try it about dusk some evening when the trout are rising to a fresh hatch and you'll instantly recognize the merits.

The tippets with the flies can be stored in small plastic envelopes or boxes (for dry flies), marked on the outside with tippet strength and fly pattern. A felt-tip marker is all you need. That way, you can be fishing again in less than a minute instead of struggling to locate the right pattern and then going blind trying to tie it on.

At this point, you might agree that the idea sounds great in theory, but question the effect of the loop system on the fish-catching ability of a delicate tippet. The same thought bothered us, so we did a great deal of comparative fishing. We found that the loops had no effect on trout (or any other species) even with tippets as fine as 6X or 7X. And we used the same system on Atlantic salmon with equally rewarding success. It works and it catches fish, providing you are skilled in the basics of fly fishing and can present a fly in a natural manner.

Most anglers question this method when fishing dry flies. They reason that they can "get away with it" if they use streamers or wets, but consider dries to be the real test. Actually, when fishing dry flies, the diameter of the leader tippet and the method of connecting the leader sections is far less important to the fish than a drag-free float. Drag on the water seems to be the main reason trout ignore an offering.

STANDARD SALTWATER FLY LEADER

The standard saltwater fly leader must meet three requirements. Since your quarry will be bigger and tougher than almost any fresh water species, you must have 100% knot strength so that you can apply maximum pressure when fighting a fish. You are also faced with the problem of making a swift and accurate presentation to a fish, and then you must concern yourself with landing a rugged adversary.

Serious saltwater fly rodders shun ready-made leaders, favoring only those they can tie themselves. Most leaders on the market today do not have a sufficiently heavy butt section to transmit energy from the fly line to the fly. The tippet section on these leaders is not long enough, and a complete taper is seldom necessary.

If you intend to enter a fish for record purposes, your leader must be at least six feet long in salt water, with a tippet section a minimum of twelve inches long. You are permitted to add a shock tippet of any material, providing it does not exceed twelve inches in length. Recognized categories in salt water are six-, ten-, twelve-, and fifteen-pound test, measured at wet strength. No contest or record keeping organization will honor a tippet that exceeds fifteen-pound test and many require that the tippet be no more than twelve-pound test.

In a saltwater fly leader, the butt section is usually about two-thirds of the total leader length. This is fashioned from a single strand of thirty- or forty-pound test monofilament and attached to the fly line with a Needle Knot or Nail Knot. The fly-line attachment should be coated with a rubber-base cement such as Pliobond to insure that it will slide through the rod guides easily and without catching. Since most saltwater leaders range between six and nine feet, the butt section varies from four to six feet depending on desired total leader length.

There are two reasons for this unusually long butt section. You will be casting heavy, wind-resistant flies and the beefed-up butt section will help to carry the weight of these flies. More important, this is also a fish-fighting leader. To bring a fish close to the boat, you'll have to reel part of the leader through the guides. If the leader were knotted as much as a normally tapered leader is, you would stand a chance of catching a knot in the guides and breaking the leader. The long, heavy butt section enables you to bring two-thirds of the leader through the guides before you reach the next connection.

When you have connected the butt section to the fly line, tie a Double Surgeon's Loop in the fishing end of the butt section. There is no gradual taper. Instead, the tippet section is attached directly to the butt section. You will jump, for example, from a thirty-pound butt section to a twelve-pound tippet section.

STANDARD SALT WATER LEADER

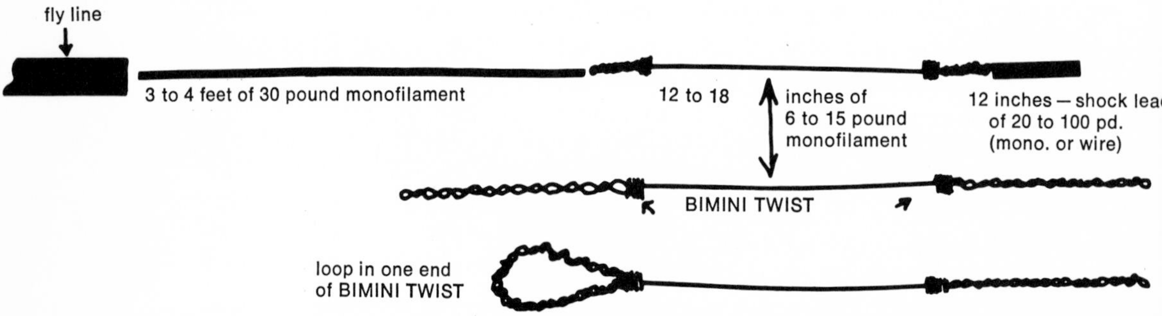

fly line
3 to 4 feet of 30 pound monofilament
12 to 18 inches of 6 to 15 pound monofilament
12 inches — shock lea[der] of 20 to 100 pd. (mono. or wire)
BIMINI TWIST
loop in one end of BIMINI TWIST

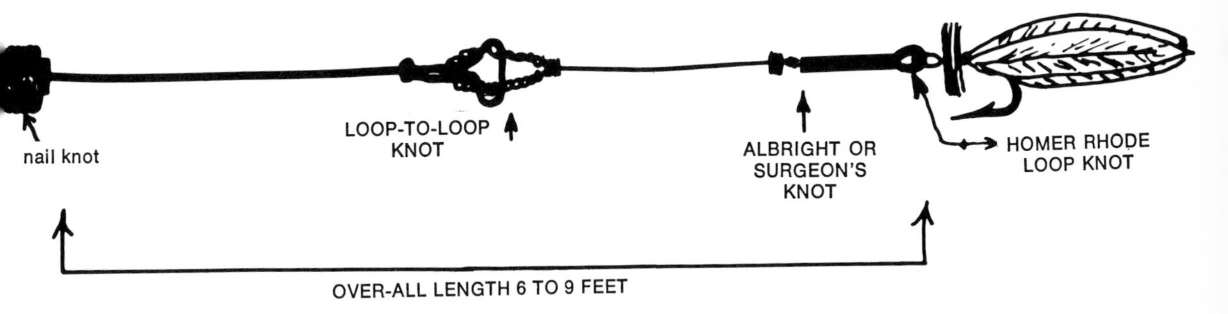

Making up the tippet section will take a little time. Spool off a length of monofilament in the breaking strength you prefer within the six-to-fifteen-pound-test limitations and tie a Bimini Twist in each end. If you intend to live up to the rules of saltwater fly rodding, the single strand of tippet *between* the two Bimini Twists must be at least twelve inches long. Rather than make this strand exactly twelve inches, we prefer to vary the length of the tippet between twelve and thirty inches depending on its breaking strength. Our own research over the years has demonstrated that *the lighter the tippet strength, the longer the tippet.* That is, if you are using six-pound test, you should have a tippet length of thirty inches. Ten- and twelve-pound tippets would have lengths between twelve and twenty-four inches.

The reason for the difference in lengths is to take advantage of the amount of stretch built into monofilament. Stretch is a cushion and it is forgiving if you make a miscalculation in the amount of pressure you apply. There is slightly more stretch in eighteen inches of monofilament than there is in twelve inches, but every little bit helps. With very light tippets such as six-pound test, these few inches of extra monofilament can spell the difference. And if you remember from an earlier chapter, impact strength is related to the length of line. So if you have more line (or in this case, a longer tippet), the impact can be spread over a longer length.

When you have tied a Bimini Twist in each end of the tippet, allowing the proper length between the two knots, you are ready for the next step. Double over one of the Bimini Twists (creating four strands of line) and tie a Double Surgeon's Loop using all four strands. This loop is then interlocked with the one in the butt section of the leader using a Loop-to-Loop Knot.

A twelve-inch shock tippet of either monofilament or wire is generally added to the regular tippet for protection against abrasion or sharp teeth. The shock tippet ranges in breaking strength from twenty to one hundred pounds depending upon the species you expect to catch. If you select single-strand wire, the attachment to the monofilament is made with an Albright Knot. For plastic-coated wire or monofilament, you have a choice of either the Albright Knot or the Double Surgeon's Knot. The fly is connected with a Homer Rhode Loop Knot or a Duncan Loop. With plastic-coated wire, you may also use the Heated Twist. Single-strand solid wire dictates a Haywire Twist when connecting to the fly.

There are a few situations in salt water where a delicate presentation is paramount. Tailing bonefish in a few inches of water is the textbook example. In that case, you would not use a shock leader. In fact, because of the delicate presentation required, you would probably use a leader that is twelve to fifteen feet long and tapered very much like a freshwater leader.

Saltwater fish are often on the move and, when action comes, it comes fast. Making up a saltwater leader on the water with fish all around can become a frustrating experience because of the number of knots required. Since you are using interlocking loops to connect the leader to the butt section, the entire leader can be made up in advance. We prefer to tie a fly on the end of each leader and then store it in a plastic bag marked with the contents. Each leader-and-fly combination goes in a separate plastic bag. When we want to change flies or if a fish just broke off, we can be back in action in a matter of seconds. The old tippet section is discarded and a new leader with fly attached is looped to the butt section.

If you're not certain about the fly patterns you are going to use or the breaking strength of the shock tippet, you can still save time by making up part of the leader in advance. Take an empty line spool for each breaking strength of tippet you use. When time permits at home, while commuting to work, or while traveling, you can make up a few dozen tippet sections in each breaking strength. All you have to do is tie a Bimini Twist in both ends and then a Double Surgeon's Loop in one end. Loosely interlock the loops between each tippet and wind them on the empty line spool (correctly marked with breaking strength). Carry these spools with you when you are fishing. If you have to tie a new leader, you have most of it already done. Simply loop the Double Surgeon's Loop to the butt section, tie on the shock tippet, and then the fly.

LEADERS FOR CASTING TACKLE

Whether you use spinning, bait casting, or larger conventional casting tackle, there are times when you will require a leader system. The surf caster, for example, faces the problem of snapping light lines on the cast because of the power generated through the longer rods customarily used in that phase of the sport. A heavier shock leader to absorb the snap of the cast is the answer and it can be formed in two ways. You can tie a long Bimini Twist in the end of the casting line or use a length of heavier monofilament.

The shock leader for surf casting should be longer than the length of the rod and provide enough length so that you can have three or four turns of the heavier line on the reel before you cast. If you use only the Bimini Twist, you will need someone to help you tie it, because it will be far too long to

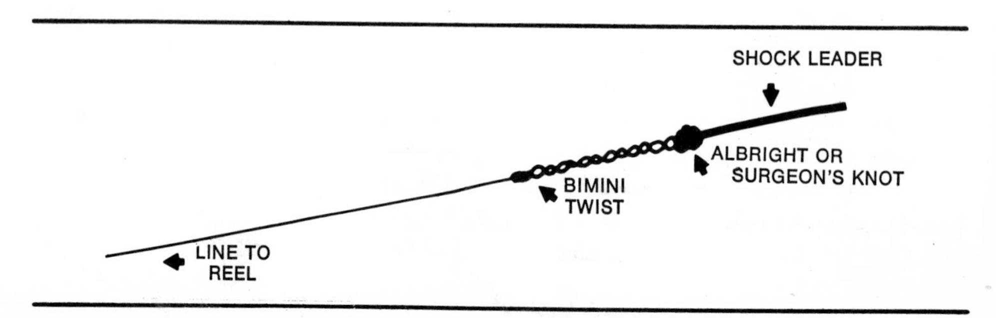

place over your knees. If you prefer a length of heavier monofilament, tie a Bimini Twist in the end of the casting line. Then attach the shock leader to the Bimini with a Surgeon's Knot or an Albright. This will provide 100% leader strength when fighting a fish and it will solve the problem of breaking the lighter line on the cast.

Except for surf casting with longer rods, the problem of breaking the line on the cast (providing the lure is free) does not occur frequently. If you are having trouble with lines breaking, check your line to see if it should be replaced and check the guides and tip-top of the rod to make sure they are not nicked or grooved. Otherwise, you may be casting incorrectly. However, the same system used by the surf caster could apply to other types of casting tackle if you feel it is necessary.

The casting enthusiast often requires a leader system for protection against abrasion or species with sharp teeth. Every leader system should start with a Bimini Twist in the end of the casting line. Then, it's a matter of building the type of leader you need. If you are concerned about a fish's teeth biting through the leader or the line, you won't need a very long shock leader. But in those situations where abrasion is the problem, the leader system should be longer.

The basic leader system is primarily the same regardless of species. If you simply need a short leader of wire or mono, it is tied directly to the Bimini Twist with an Albright Knot or a Surgeon's Knot. Single-strand solid wire dictates a short length of heavier monofilament attached to the Bimini Twist before making the Albright.

For tarpon, sharks, deep jigging, and other situations where you would require a longer leader for abrasion protection, you can use two strengths of monofilament. Start with the Bimini Twist and attach a length of twenty- or thirty-pound test monofilament. Then, connect this medium weight mono to whatever shock tippet you require. Once you learn the basic system, it can be modified to work in fresh water or salt for any species of fish.

OFFSHORE LEADERS

The blue-water troller has his own system for making leaders and it starts with a Bimini Twist. The Bimini was originally an offshore knot for tying a double line long before someone decided that it just might work on casting tackle. The double line for trolling is usually fifteen feet long (thirty feet with heavy-class tackle) and it is formed by tying a Bimini Twist. A swivel is tied on the end of the Bimini with an Offshore Swivel Knot.

Single-strand solid wire and aircraft cable have been the standbys of the deep water fishing fraternity. Solid wire is used for smaller species and the cable is employed for giant billfish. These are looped on one end and simply hung on the swivel. The other end is tied to the hook. In the last few years, however, experienced trollers have been abandoning the wire in favor of heavy monofilament wherever species and circumstances permit. Monofilament leaders are even being used for sailfish and white marlin because anglers feel they get more strikes and raise more fish than they do with wire. Larger billfish such as blue marlin, black marlin, and striped marlin still require cable.

Certain offshore bait-rigging techniques could present a problem with monofilament leaders, because the bait rigging is done with solid wire. But this is easy to overcome. Anglers still rig the baits with wire, but they attach a swivel or simply put a Haywire Twist Loop in the wire right after it leaves the bait. Then they attach the monofilament leader to the short length of wire.

Monofilament leaders also present an advantage for the new breed of offshore angler who goes to sea in small boats. Trying to handle fifteen feet of wire in a miniature rig can be a problem at sea. Even if you need wire, use only a few feet. Then make the rest of your leader monofilament. That way, the mono can be handled easily aboard a small boat.

Anyone who has done some offshore fishing knows that the policy is to make up all the leaders in advance so that they are ready to go at a moment's notice. It's a good practice to follow.

LEADERS FOR NATURAL BAIT FISHING

Leaders for bait fishing are so varied that it would be impossible to list and illustrate all of them. You'll find that the same species in different areas is fished with different rigs. Local preferences and even your own experience play a large part in the way you will rig. On the other hand, if you learn the basic knots in this book, you should be able to construct any leader required.

Whenever possible, start with a Bimini Twist in the end of the line. Then, construct the leader system from that point and you shouldn't have any problems. You should be able to select the strongest knots for tying to a hook, swivel, or sinker. And there are several ways illustrated for making loops.

Whether you fish freshwater or salt, you won't have trouble fashioning any leader required as long as you favor those knots with the highest-rated breaking strengths. The key to any leader lies in the knots used rather than the basic leader design.